WHO'S ON FIRST

Novels by William F. Buckley, Jr.

    WHO'S ON FIRST
    STAINED GLASS
    SAVING THE QUEEN

William F. Buckley, Jr.

WHO'S ON FIRST

Doubleday & Company, Inc., GARDEN CITY, NEW YORK

This is a work of fiction. Some of the figures who appear, however, do so under their own names.

A portion of this novel originally appeared in *Playboy* magazine.

Copyright © 1980 by William F. Buckley, Jr.
PRINTED IN THE UNITED STATES OF AMERICA
ALL RIGHTS RESERVED

For *Dino John Pionzio*

What were the terrible 1960s and where did they come from? To begin with, the 1960s did not start in 1960. They started in 1957. A bell rings in my mind every time I hear the date 1957 mentioned. On October 4, 1957, the Russians placed a medicine-ball-sized satellite in orbit. It needs an effort to remember how stunned we were when we discovered that the clodhopping Russians were technologically ahead of us, and that we would have to catch up with them. We reacted hysterically.

Before the Sabbath
Eric Hoffer, 1979

A: Now, on the St. Louis team we have Who's on first, What's on second, I Don't Know is on third—
C: That's what I want to find out—
A: I'm telling you. Who's on first, What's on second, I Don't Know is on third—
C: Well all I'm trying to find out is what's the guy's name on first base.
A: Oh, no, no, What's on second base.
C: I'm not asking you who's on second.
A: Who's on first.
C: That's what I'm trying to find out.
A: Well, don't change the players around.
C: I'm not changing nobody.
A: Now, take it easy.
C: What's the guy's name on first base?
A: What's the guy's name on second base.
C: I'm not askin' ya who's on second.
A: Who's on first.
C: I don't know.
A: Please. Now what is it you want to know?
C: What is the fellow's name on third base?
A: What is the fellow's name on second base.
C: I'm not askin' ya who's on second.
A: Who's on first.
C: I don't know.

Abbott and Costello

WHO'S ON FIRST

Chapter 1

HE HEARD THE ROAR of an oncoming truck. The noise broke the silence of his fourth-floor apartment on Dohany Street. It was the first sound of a motor vehicle he had heard since late in the afternoon of the preceding day, when, finally, the last sniper's shot was fired. The last, he gathered from the shortwave radio, of the resistance in Budapest.

During the breath-catching days of liberty—one full week, the high emotional point reached with the elated release from prison of Cardinal Mindszenty on Wednesday—rumors had swept Budapest that the Russian Army was grouping for an assault. But optimism had been overwhelming: Russian tank drivers would refuse to fire on the students . . . The Secretary-General of the United Nations would fly in to abort any attempted Soviet military reoccupation . . . The people of the other satellite states were in open revolt . . . Khrushchev would call back his divisions from Eastern Europe before the week was out.

When the Russians did move—with eight divisions—at 4 A.M. on Friday, the protests poured in from European capitals. The Security Council was convened at three in the morning, New York time. President Eisenhower publicly deplored the turn of events. But the voice of BBC soon lost that flush of excitement, and the announcers once again sounded—Blackford Oakes recalled George Orwell's phrase—"genteel and throaty"—as they acknowledged the fall of Budapest and the "desultory resistance" in the countryside. The BBC attempted to coordinate transmissions from pockets of resistance, relaying directly broadcasts from the freedom fighters who had begun by using government facilities—they controlled them: They were, were they not, the legal government of Hungary? When the Communists, with their unerring eye for the ganglia, seized the radio stations, the broadcasts resumed from shortwave transmission sets secreted in the outskirts of the city, and in the country. These dwindled in number, and then there was that last haunting voice at 0924 which had addressed the outside world and ended with the simple words "Help! Help! Help!" It was fifteen minutes after midnight when broadcasting resumed, and the Hungarians informed that they had been saved from "the rebirth of fascism."

Blackford Oakes sat in a stuffed easy chair, in the little suite at the Hotel Sarkany with the heavy furniture, which once was red, perhaps the same color as the heavy drapes, though over the generations their colors had polarized. Now the ample couch and armchairs were a dirty brown, the sun-bombarded curtains an anemic pink, the carpet just that shade of gray designed to conceal dirt of almost any hue, a rectangular section of it, shaded by the husky oak table he used as a desk and to eat from, darker than the surrounding area in the congested little living room, where Blackford reflected mordantly on the comforts of home during other people's carnage. But the window was imposing, as if once it had served grander purposes: Perhaps a larger room had been subdivided. He could adjust the venetian blinds and see out clearly; or he could turn the latch and draw open by as little or as much as he wanted, one-half the vaulted glass, and run his eyes up the ancient Gothic street, cobblestoned, of medium width, lined with shops and apartment houses; closed now, though three days had passed since the fateful Sunday morning when the troops and the tanks came. They alone had come; no one else. The leader of the free world, as people liked to call him, and as he was not entirely averse occasionally to calling himself, was apoplectic. But not about the Russians. About the British and the French, who had elected the week before to invade the Suez, bound ostensibly for Cairo. Besides, only yesterday he had been recrowned by the American voters, and today, Wednesday, he was expected to fly to

Denver for a little golf. How how how, Oakes wondered, could providence have been so perverse as to synchronize a rebellion for freedom with a venture that would be denounced as imperialism? Yes, from the office of the stricken British Prime Minister reproaches were directed at the Soviet Government, which heard also from the French. But the Soviet press swiftly retaliated with denunciations of British-French imperialism. The American Secretary of State was so overwhelmed with frustration by the furtive operation in the Mideast mounted by our closest friends, without consultation, that he had had to be hospitalized. So that as it happened, nothing emanating from the White House or the State Department would have stopped a Russian ballet, let alone two hundred Russian tanks. The American ambassador at the U.N. uttered a sharp rebuke. Oakes could imagine Khrushchev and Gromyko playing games the Sunday before—Khrushchev liked that sort of thing, though he was heavy-handed—imitating the excoriations from the West, including gestures. Gromyko, Oakes thought, reaching back over thirteen years' experience at, or near, the top of the Soviet diplomatic establishment, would say: "The more emphasis the Americans put on the U.N., comrade, the less we have to worry about."

Oakes's ruminations were interrupted as the sound of the motor got louder, and he rose and opened the window discreetly to look down the street, in the direction it came from. He saw leading the column a jeep with four men, the civilian next to the driver holding in his hand a clipboard. Behind him two officers, one of them studying a map spread out over his knees. There followed a half-track armored car, six soldiers with machine guns seated on the platform to the rear of the heavily armored driver's cabin. There rose from the same platform what looked like a small gantry. Swinging coquettishly from it—Oakes stopped breathing—was a clearly discernible noose. Instantly his eyes turned to the building across the street, two doors down. *Theo!*—the word formed itself in his throat. But no. The room in the quiet old boardinghouse, the small, tidy room maintained by the little salesman who regularly paid the rent but was seldom there, was surely inviolate. When on the Wednesday night two weeks ago young Theo told him the action was about to begin, Oakes had made a human gesture. "If it goes sour, you'll be safe." Had Theo taken refuge there? Theo had taken to sleeping at Frieda's house whenever Frieda's mother was in Vác, looking after her orphaned nephew and niece. Perhaps Theo was hiding at Frieda's. Perhaps he had been captured.

Oakes remembered the utter elation in the young student's face when he met Blackford at the tavern, during the tense week before the assumption of power by Imre Nagy. At twenty, Theophilus Molnar was slight of build, but the star soccer player at the university. His fingers were slender and his voice had a premature gentleness, that of a philosopher who, along the way, decides that, really, there is nothing left in the world worth raising one's voice about. His excitement was internalized. Theo knew Blackford Oakes as a young engineer hired by an Austrian firm to be the purchasing agent for special American equipment required to construct the huge new municipal aquarium. They met first irregularly, and then two or three times a week, usually at the same tavern, a favorite of the students and the younger teachers. At first Theo talked mostly about the soccer games, occasionally about his absorption in classical studies: but gradually about his determination, and that of his friends, to strike out and free their country from the Soviet Union. One night he introduced Frieda, almost as tall as Theo, with bright eyes and intense manner, passionate in her convictions, inquisitive about Blackford, exultant over her command of English, so much more fluent than her fiancé's. She laughed a lot, her political passion notwithstanding, and the hours went quickly as they had beer, and chicken, and peasant bread, and tea, since coffee was rare. Always, as summer turned to fall, the conversation would turn to the imminent emancipation of Hungary, and of Theo's and Frieda's plans. They would travel the following summer. Might they visit Harry—as they knew him—in the United States? Theo had a maiden aunt, he told Harry, who had divulged to him where she kept gold she had hoarded beginning when she started to work during World War II, and it would be his when she died; and she was very feeble, at seventy-six. She was a woman of great thrift, Theo explained, and although she had never specified how much gold she actually had, she loved to tell him that it would all be his, "so you can travel, anywhere you want, before you become a professor of Greek or whatever it is you are doing," Theo imitated his aunt's prim accent. "I will marry Frieda first," he said—"and you, Harry, will you come to my wedding? For a wedding present, you can give Frieda and me an aquarium." "Just a little aquarium, Harry," Frieda interrupted, holding Theo's hand across the table. But it all depended, Theo said, on the success of the great venture ahead of them. His almond-shaped eyes would light up at every mention of the prospective freedom about which at first he fantasized cautiously. He spoke usually in German, occasionally in a lilting English into which he effortlessly insinuated the German when he did not know the English word. He had told Harry that their plans were not mere abstractions. That they intended to take power. How? By actually forcing the resignation of the satellite Prime Minister and replacing him with a patriot. What would the Russians do? The Russians, he explained earnestly, his dark hair falling down loosely over his young, unlined forehead, could not *hope* to hang on to the satellite empire. Theo spoke in his still, soft way, playing with a breadstick, which he looked down at as he whispered discreetly. The Russians, he reminded Blackford, had had troubles earlier on in the year in Poland. Czechoslovakia was restive. Bulgaria and Romania would be tougher to pry loose, and East Germany probably the last to assert itself. But—he smiled, showing his small, even teeth; a smile with the assurance distinctive to the truly innocent—the Russians would accept *fatalistically* the nationalism that was about to take over. Stalin was dead. He had been denounced only eight months ago by Khrushchev himself. Khrushchev had spoken of a thaw and released millions of prisoners. It is God's will, Theo said, that man should be free. The emancipation of the satellites was a necessary next step, didn't Harry think so?

Blackford Oakes, taller than Theo by several inches, older by eleven years, with hair lingeringly blond, his blue eyes expressive, the tiniest crease of experience visible at the corners, bore himself in the relaxed manner of the perfectly proportioned young American male, totally relaxed physically. But he replied in a voice tenser than Theo was used to hearing: "Don't count on it."

"Wouldn't the Americans help?"

"What could they do?"

"What could they *do?* Harry, what could they *do!* The Americans control the world! One word from the White House and that's it!"

"Theo. Listen. Listen hard. If One Word from the White House were all that was needed to free Hungary, that word would have been uttered a long time ago. The White House can't give any words until internal conditions are ripe."

"What I'm telling you," Theo said excitedly, "is that those conditions are ripe *right now*. I meet twice a week with . . ." He paused. Embarrassed, Theo looked down at the breadstick and finished his interrupted sentence ". . . people. People who know. The Americans won't make the mistake of missing *this* signal. It will be *very* clear."

"But Theo. What if the White House gives the magic word and the Russians ignore it?"

"There will be chaos, stretching from Danzig to Trieste. The Russians can't contend with chaos."

Blackford said nothing. Then he thought, and spoke quietly, but the tone of voice was decisive: "Be careful about yourself. Now repeat this." Theo looked up, curious, tense, silent. "Repeat after me: 41 Dohany Street, Room 4C." Theo understood, and his clean-shaven face was perfectly solemn when he said, as though an acolyte, "41 Dohany, Room 4C."

"Don't mention that address to anybody."

"I won't."

Blackford rose and shook hands. Theo felt the slim cold object, and deftly he slipped the key unobserved into his pants pocket. Three days later Nagy made his move, two days later the statue of Stalin was ripped down from its imperious domination of the Kossuth Square, to the shouts and cheers of what must have been half the population of Budapest, though not including Blackford Oakes, who had been given strict instructions not to move from his hotel in the event. . . .

* * *

Blackford closed his eyes briefly and prayed that the convoy would pass by. The lead jeep stopped twenty meters down the road to his right and the soldiers jumped out and deployed opposite 41 Dohany. A detail of three men approached the entrance. Finding the door locked, the leader first rang the bell, then banged on the door, motioning one of his men to enter the abutting building, giving him instructions Blackford could hear distinctly, but did not understand. In a moment a white-haired woman dressed in black and wearing a white apron opened the door, stiffened, and stepped back. The officer pushed her to one side and, followed by his subordinates, charged into the building. There was a silence. Ten seconds? Thirty seconds? A single shot rang out. The soldiers in the street tensed. Crouched behind their weapons, they looked like statues in a war memorial. Two minutes later the detail filed out, dragging their quarry, who was dressed in faded brown corduroys and a blue shirt, his pale hands tied behind him. Although Theo had evidently not shaved in a day or more, his face still looked like that of a growing boy. The official dressed in civilian clothes stepped down from the jeep, adjusted his spectacles, and read out loud from his clipboard in a humdrum voice three or four paragraphs from which Oakes recognized only the words "Theophilus Molnar." He was led forthwith to the back of the half-track and hoisted by the shoulders to the platform. Blackford was not thirty-five feet from him. Theo's face was calm, his eyes closed. Now he raised his eyes and spoke in his soft voice to the senior officer. It must have been a request, because the answer was unmistakably negative. The assistant adjusted the noose around Theo's neck, and shouted out to the driver, and Blackford heard a gear engage. Whereupon, slowly, the hydraulic motor racing, the long arm of the portable crane began to rise, tugging up, slowly, the body of Theophilus Molnar, which, when his toes left the platform, began convulsively to thrash about, a whine of sorts issuing from the throat. Blackford had seen him play soccer, and the hideous parallel in the physical body motions, at play and in death, convulsed him. It required over three minutes before the twirling line hung down straight again, the boy's head bent over like the end of a shaggy black mop. A soldier pulled, from a stack of identical placards banked at the forward end of the platform, one on which had been printed certain words in Hungarian. He exhibited the placard to the half-dozen silent witnesses who had ventured out of their houses, and then tied it about Theo's waist with a coarse line he handled like apron strings. The order went out, and the convoy resumed its promenade down the street, Theo's body a mobile exhibit. The officer in the back seat was staring again at the map.

Blackford Oakes went to his door, unlocked it, and walked down the staircase to the concierge. He asked hoarsely: "What does the sign say?"

"Death to counterrevolutionaries."

"What did . . . the young man ask the officer?"

"If he might be permitted to make the Sign of the Cross."

Chapter 2

ALTHOUGH IT HAD been four years since he served as Secretary of State, he still used a limousine. Indeed it would have been easier to imagine Queen Victoria changing the tire of her car than Dean Acheson climbing out of a taxi, let alone driving himself to the old house in Georgetown which he had visited so frequently when his duties were official. For an interval, the Director of Central Intelligence, a Republican, had observed the mandate of the election of 1952 with punctilio, and so for a year or two the two men, who had conferred on so many crises, saw less of each other. But notwithstanding that his own (*extremely* Republican) brother was now the incumbent Secretary of State, the Director found himself missing the mordant analyses and geopolitical clairvoyance of this infuriating man, who had recently published a book called *A Democrat Looks at His Party,* in which he had calmly announced that the distinction between a Republican and a Democrat is that Democrats tend to be bright and Republicans tend to be stupid.

"It's just that easy," he now told the Director at tea. "You mustn't be offended by this, Allen. Besides, you must find it consoling that your people will stay in power a good long time." This conversation, taking place two months after the Democrats sacrificed for the second time the most conspicuous egghead in the Democratic party in the election against the universally popular liberator of Europe, there was a special sense of resignation in the fateful observation.

"In some discursive reading the other day," the former Secretary went on, "I found interesting collaboration for this thesis. It is from a speech by John Stuart Mill delivered, I believe, in the British Parliament." With his left hand he extended his teacup to the maid, who refilled it as he adjusted his glasses with his right hand.

"Mill said, 'I never meant to say that the Conservatives are generally stupid. I meant to say that stupid people are generally Conservative. I believe that is so obviously and universally admitted a principle'"—the Secretary raised his eyebrows in obeisance to the majesty of First Principles—"'that I hardly think any gentleman will deny it. Suppose any party, in addition to whatever share it may possess of the ability of the community, had nearly the whole of its stupidity, that party must'—take heart, Allen!—'by the laws of its constitution, be the stupidest party; and I do not see why honorable gentlemen should see that position as at all offensive to them, for it ensures their being always an extremely powerful party.'"

He smiled with great satisfaction and looked up again, as if to acknowledge yet another providential insight.

The Director was more phlegmatic than his older brother, who would have retaliated massively. Allen Dulles satisfied himself with grunting: "If we had had one more brain at Yalta and Potsdam, Dean, the Russians would have got Westminster Abbey."

Four times, during the explosive events of October and November, they had met; and although the Secretary of State knew of these meetings and took discreet reassurance from the knowledge that his predecessor, whom he had come secretly to admire, was being regularly consulted by no less trustworthy a man than the Secretary of State's own brother, under no circumstances would the Secretary have participated in any of them, no more than he would have invited the brainy Democrat to the White House whose tenant had, in any event, always been ill at ease with Acheson. "To put up with Acheson," the Director's deputy had once observed, "you have to be terribly bright and suave, or a political gunslinger governed by his gonads. Nothing in between. What we have in the White House is in between."

The visit was early in January, before the President's State of the Union message. Outside it was wet gray snow, something like the national mood. "You will need," Acheson said, stirring his tea, "to reformulate a foreign policy. The old business about 'liberating Eastern Europe' is no longer very persuasive."

"It may not be, but you're not going to hear anything very different. Only the formulation is scheduled to change. We will be talking about 'liberation by evolution.' That's the ticket."

"May I presume to suggest that that particular speech be delivered in the United Nations? The two were meant for each other."

The Director smiled, while puffing on his pipe, as if on the homestretch to orgasm. Pause. Then: "It's not decided when or where. The timing *is* of some importance. The U.S. needs a leg up in international public opinion. It would be good if that declaration were to coincide with something that would resurrect our prestige."

"I hate to say it, Allen, but you are really suggesting the resignation of your brother."

The Director never rose to the fraternal bait. He smiled diplomatically, and went on. "We have something else in mind."

"May I inquire?"

"We want an artificial satellite—before they get one. Beginning July 1, 1957, we get the eighteen-month International Geophysical Year, and our idea is to celebrate it with a satellite. The satellite is more than a stunt, as you no doubt know. Satellites will be able to see. See a bucket of water in an open field. They will open the scientific door to pinpoint ICBMs. They are the key to the next, probably definitive, generation of strategic weapons. But *launching* that first satellite is the ticket, as far as the military people are concerned—they know where to head, from that point on, with a reliable missile system. An orbiting satellite, the scientists know, simply validates the truism that the gravitational pull of the earth plus a complementary speed equals something on the order of a perpetual satellite."

"How're we doing?"

"We've got problems. So do they. What we haven't got a line on is just what their problems are, and how we can help make them worse. We're talking eight, ten, twelve months away, our people figure. But whenever: The world's first satellite has *got* to be launched from Cape Canaveral."

The former Secretary put down his cup. "If we can't beat them at the scientific level, we *are* in a bad way. Can't we hire enough Germans to do it for us?"

"Most of the Germans with rocket experience were whisked off to Moscow. During *your* administration, Dean. You might call it 'The Brains' Brain Drain.' "

"Allen, you are getting polemical, and since you're not as good at it as I am, I suggest you mind your manners."

Dulles ignored the taunt. "We did get Von Braun. And he's working full-time. But our job—the Agency's job—isn't to help Von Braun. That's for the Defense Department and related agencies. Our job is to hamstring the Reds, and we don't know how to go about it, because we don't know (a) what it is they need most, (b) whether we're in a position to keep them from getting it, whatever it is, or—(c) for how long we can keep it from them if we can isolate their problem."

Acheson got up to go. "Let me think about it. Have you got any *good* news?"

"Jean-Paul Sartre gave a speech yesterday denouncing the Communists for invading Hungary and canceling his membership in the party."

"Good news? Sartre turning to the West? We have enough problems."

The Director smiled. "He has his following, Dean."

"I suppose. Unlike your nephew, I've resisted any temptation to Romanism but the nearest I ever came to Poping was when the Vatican put Sartre on the Index." He picked up his umbrella after fastening his coat. "As it is, my gesture to ecumenism is to obey the Index on Sartre. Good afternoon, Allen."

"Bye-bye, Dean."

The two men parted at the door, shaking hands.

Chapter 3

"WHAT WERE YOU actually *doing* in Budapest?" Sally asked as she poured him the gin and tonic from the kitchen shelf.

"Sally?"

"Yes, Blacky."

"Put a touch of Campari in that, will you? Something I learned from an Argentinian steward."

"Did he get killed for telling you?"

Blackford managed a grin, but at the same time he sprang up distractedly from the sofa on which he had been characteristically draped, and walked toward the teeming bookshelf of the small apartment, without answering.

"I said, Blacky, what actually were you doing in Budapest?" Her teasing, seductive coloratura sang through the open door.

"Sally dear, your curiosity is supposed to carry you up through the first . . . third of the nineteenth century. When exactly *did* Jane Austen die?"

"1867."

Blackford paused.

"Oh yes, of course, I remember now. She died of grief over Seward's Folly in purchasing Alaska."

"Funny."

"Look, Sally." His hand played with her light brown hair, and she moved her head to acknowledge the caress. "You're not supposed to know how to build a bridge, like us engineers; but us engineers *are* supposed to have some idea when Jane Austen died, so cut the crap, okay? When *did* she die?"

"1817. What's the point?"

Blackford resumed his inspection of the bookshelves. He delayed in answering.

"Oh, I forgot," he said, slumping down again on the couch and extending his hand to receive the proffered drink. "I guess I was going to say that because you now have yourself a Ph.D. based on your knowledge of the Life and Times of J. Austen, this shouldn't suggest to you that you're omniscient on the matter of the life and times of Joseph Stalin—(when did Stalin die, darling?)—or his choirboys who moved into Budapest. What was *I* doing? Sally, you've known now for five years the business I'm in, and for five years you've known I can't tell you what I do, so why ask?"

She moved beside him and sat on the arm of the couch, and whispered, "Blacky darling, you're the loveliest man I ever met, and it isn't like you to be irritable. That's happening to you because of your involvement in . . . in this *sordid mess*." He thought: if only she knew how sordid it was. And then, impetuously, though he had solemnly resolved he wouldn't do so, he told her—about Theo.

He could scarcely get through it, and in the end he was hoarse, and there were tears.

"You see, his last thought—hell, *one* of his last thoughts, God knows how many one can have in the three minutes—one hundred and eighty seconds—it takes to strangle—one of his last thoughts must have been that *I* was one of *them*. How else would the KGB have got hold of the address of the Safe House? I've thought about it. I've built calculuses of probability. Cathedrals of logic. I've catalogued every explanation I could think of. Theo concluded either that I was a traitor; or if not, that I was a sympathizer who confessed, or was tortured into giving up my secrets; or that I was careless, and let the information get out. They drove right to his fucking house *as if they'd come to escort him to his wedding!*"

Sally asked softly, "How *did* they know?"

"I damn near blew the place apart trying to find out. You know something? The arrangements at that boardinghouse were made *by me* personally. The cash payments were made every two months by a Hungarian contact who lived in the suburbs, a guy we had worked with for years. I got out there, two days later—had to show my phony papers at two checkpoints—ready to kill the son of a bitch. I knocked on the door and demanded to see him. His wife doesn't speak German, English, or French, but she caught on. She put on a heavy shawl and beckoned me to follow her. She grabbed her daughter from the study, a girl about ten or twelve. Then she led me wordlessly—I just followed her—six blocks away, to a cemetery, and then to two fresh graves. He had died—three weeks before the Russians came—of a heart attack, the daughter explained to me in schoolgirl English. The other grave was the girl's brother's. He was killed by the Russians during the Resistance, a day before Theo. I didn't ask her anything else, I just left her, kneeling by the graves, with her little girl, reciting a rosary."

The silence was long.

"Who did it?"

Blackford shrugged his shoulders. "In this business, you never know. Maybe the landlady got suspicious. Who knows?"

"Blacky, you've got to get out."

"I'm not going to get out."

"In that case—I'm not going to marry you."

He looked at her, without resentment. Why should she understand? The U.S. Government understood, in a geopolitical sort of way. In the same sense that one can understand that what's good for General Motors is good for America: What's good for humanity in East Europe is good for America. But only a few really understood. And many of them were immobilized by a paralyzing fatalism, like decent southerners, who lived without protest, generations after witnessing a lynching. Blackford Oakes felt only this, that there wasn't any alternative for those few who *did* understand, or thought they did. They *had,* living in the same world, to do *something.* He wanted very much to marry this intriguing, learned, beautiful woman—who went frequently to meetings of the Sane Nuclear Policy Committee, who talked fervently of disarmament, and the lessening of international tensions, and of the great thaw that had resulted from the death of the abnormal Stalin, and of how the U.N. was our last, best hope. There were two kinds of coexistence, he saw. One with *them,* two-scorpions-in-a-bottle sort of thing. And coexistence with people like Sally, who wouldn't step on a scorpion, for fear of causing pain. His impulse, *at this very moment,* was to march with her to the altar and to swear before God that he would live with her as one person, and love and protect her, in sickness and in health, till death did them part. Why not? Budapest was *four thousand miles* away. This business of being involved in mankind was just too goddam much. If he could keep his distance from Tobacco Road, couldn't he leave *Budapest* be, let alone *Moscow?* He took her hand and leaned up, to kiss her gently, above the eye. Suddenly his mood changed, and he felt a general elation as the parts came together; the concept of integrated coexistence. He brought her close to him and said: "Whenever you say, I'll wait for you always. But I can't disengage now on the other things. Do you understand?" "I do," she said, stroking his hair. They sat there silently for a long period. The late afternoon became early evening. The apartment became dark.

Suddenly he looked up, his boyish face bright with the ingenuity of it all: "Ah," he said, "let's move into the bedroom! Better light. . . ."

She turned her head to one side, and he thought he had never seen such lovely hair.

"No, Blacky," she said softly, "I won't need much light . . . to read to you from Jane Austen."

Chapter 4

THE DIRECTOR and his aide Jerry Adams got out of the car and buried their faces in woolen scarves as they walked the thirty yards up from the driveway to the ski lodge. They might have done so in any weather but, under the frigid circumstances, if anybody was observing them such a decision would have appeared logical, in the bitter cold of Stowe, Vermont, against an easterly that howled down the mountainside on which the comfortable lodge abutted, a single light in the kitchen holding out against the blackness. Moreover, if somebody had been lying in wait in a parked car, he in turn would probably have been spotted by the two occupants of another car that, passing the driveway, at nonchalant speed, continued down the road—so lonely, after dark, all the skiers having long since retreated to their caravansaries dotted about the mountain and village.

The second car drove the half mile to the chair lift and anyone observing it would assume it was bound on a maintenance or logistical mission. The headlights appeared to verify that the scene was abandoned, and so they paused at the lift, got out of the car, entered the building through the skiers' passageway, disappeared from sight for a few moments as if attending to some commission or other, reentered the car two minutes later, turned it around, and drove back, stopping at the garage at the south wing of the lodge which, after Jerry unlocked the door from inside, they entered and parked. Silently one of them walked back to the Director's Chevrolet, turned the key that had been left in the ignition, and moved the car over alongside their own. Now they locked the garage doors from inside and walked into the kitchen. The Director and his aide had hung their coats and entered the lively, paneled living room, past the dining room with the counter separating it from the kitchen, and stood by the fireplace, out of sight of the kitchen and beyond the range of anyone's hearing. Jerry said, taking a heavy log from the Director, "Let me do that." He piled it on the kindling and newspaper, looked about for a match, and settled for the Director's pipe-lighter. The response was immediate and gratifying, and they both stood close-by as the flames swept up, illuminating in dancing shadows the large comfortable room to which a wealthy sportsman brought his grandchildren to ski four or five times a year, but never on those Mondays and Tuesdays marked on his calendar with an "X," after a telephone call from his old friend and classmate, the Director.

Jerry sighed. "I must say, sir, the upper class really knows how to live."

The Director's reply was oblique. "You ski?"

"Yes, sir. As a matter of fact, I used to come to Stowe every now and then from Dartmouth. I was on the ski team. We lost seven consecutive meets."

The Director was clearly not shaken by this piece of intelligence, but years in diplomacy had trained him intuitively to keep a conversation alive rather than appear abrupt or indifferent. "Bad luck, eh?"

"No sir, bad team. But we had a lot of fun. Dartmouth isn't opposed to fun. Some people there even encourage it."

"You sound nostalgic. Are you implying your present employers don't encourage it?"

"That's a pretty fair way of putting it, sir." Jerry was on his knees, taming a promiscuous log. His red hair and freckles and powerful hands were highlighted by the fire as he gripped the iron. The Director smiled. Jerry Adams had been with him five years, and knew every one of the Director's crotchets, including that appetite of his for petty complaints against Life in the CIA. Such complaints stroked the general sense of stoicism the Director thought appropriate to the profession.

"So you find yourself burdened, do you?"

"Yes, sir. Any chance of hiring more lady spies?"

"The Supreme Court hasn't got around to telling us we have to have a quota."

"How about some preemptive action?"

"Sow wild oats on your own time," said the Director, looking at his watch. "In four minutes exactly, open the door for Serge. Rufus will arrive five minutes later. They'll be cold. They've parked their cars at the inn, and they don't know each other."

Ten minutes later the three men sat about the fire while Jerry mixed drinks in the kitchen, chatting to the security men, one of whom, wearing an apron, was starting the oven, while the other decanted two bottles of wine.

"It is very good to see you, Rufus," the Director said, nodding to the portly man opposite, who had got a little balder, a little older, but whose eyes and demeanor were unchanged.

"It's fine to see you, Allen. Though you do make it difficult to stay retired."

"At sixty-two you're too young to retire. I suppose one of these days somebody will discover you. Write a book about you. After that I promise I won't call you. After that I can't even promise to *recognize* you!" (Had he overdone it? He looked out of the side of his eye. Rufus's smile was formal, but clearly he was unconcerned.)

He turned to the third man, sitting opposite the fire. He wore boots, heavy woolen trousers, and a crew-neck sweater; but even so he rubbed his hands together, as though they would never grow warm. His hair was white, his skin jaundiced, his build stocky, tough.

"You will always be cold, eh Serge?"

The reply was in a heavily accented English. "I will always be cold."

"Rufus, I am aware that you and Serge haven't met. Haven't even heard about each other, as far as I know. On what we are calling Plan 717—July 1, 1957 is the beginning of the International Geophysical Year—you will, I hope, agree to work together."

Jerry brought in the drinks, and then went back to the kitchen.

The Director addressed the Russian. "This is Rufus. All I need to tell you about him is: He's the best we have."

Then he turned to Rufus. "Three years ago, Serge defected.

Two of our top people—you know them both—spent the better part of a year with him. He has given us invaluable stuff. We're still living off a lot of it. At our end we promised him security—and to leave him alone. He owes us nothing. But we've gone over and over the 717 project, and I concluded"—now he turned again to Serge—"that you are the key to its success. *If* it will work, it will be because of you."

Neither man commented. Rufus held his drink in his hand without even pretending to sip it. Serge attacked his in half-glass bouts and in the ensuing hour the Director twice refilled the glass.

Now the Director assumed his professional stance, standing, leaning against the stone of the chimney, puffing on his pipe.

"The Communists"—he was careful, in Serge's presence, not to say "the Russians"—"are feverishly at work on a satellite. First, they *want* a rocket and experience in atmospheric flight. Accurate intercontinental missiles is the payload of the whole enterprise. Second, the Hungary business hurt them. They're pretty stoical about psychological setbacks, in the noble tradition of the Stalin-Hitler Pact; but they don't *enjoy* it."

It occurred to Rufus that when engaged in exposition the Director treated anyone present like a beginning student. Rufus had been present on the occasion when the Director, addressing Eisenhower's general staff the day before D-Day, actually instructed them on the size of a German division. He was now lecturing a Russian on Communist psychology.

"Their organs and the satellite press have been grinding away about the great achievements of the Union of Soviet Socialist Republics. Khrushchev's Twentieth Congress speech—a copy of which we got hold of and turned loose, but which was so easy to do it's obvious they didn't care—is encouraging the myth that the death of Stalin means the death of Soviet despotism. Viewed by Stalin's standards it's true that the internal situation is less capriciously totalitarian. But it's untrue that the state is any less totalist in its repression, or ravenous in its ambitions."

Rufus had to suppress a yawn. He too knew about the Soviet Union. But eventually the Director *would* get to the point.

"What they want is to destroy what they are preparing to call the 'myth of bourgeois scientific invincibility.' Our job is to prove it is *not* a myth. If the Soviets are pulling ahead, we need to know that; if we can keep them from pulling ahead, that's our priority. In either event, we need more specific knowledge than we have of the state of missile art over there. There doesn't seem to be anything we can do to speed up the program at home. The Navy announced Vanguard two years ago. It flopped, with the Viking rockets. Ike bucked the business over to the Army, with Von Braun and his beloved Redstone. Now the President himself called in Von Braun, but the guy has this teutonic thoroughness, and he doesn't like to play scientific hunches: He's got a specific launching problem he hasn't been able to crack; he wants to build, and he says January of *next year* is the earliest he thinks we can hope to go with a satellite. The President asked him would ours be the *first* satellite in space, and Von Braun shrugged his shoulders and said, 'Esk da CIA.' Which is exactly what Ike did."

"What did you tell him?"

"I told him *I* didn't know." He looked at Serge and paused. "But that I would find out."

He waited—as if expecting to be pressed to proceed. But Rufus never pressed. And Serge had had eight years of training in self-control.

"Okay, let me put it in the briefest way. There's an all-star Russian delegation going to Paris for an international scientific conference to launch the International Geophysical Year. The conference is scheduled to last five days. The plan, at one level, is quite simple. It is to . . . detach . . . one of the participants who can be counted on to have the information we want—and to get that information from him."

Rufus interrupted. "I don't do that sort of thing. I thought you knew that."

"I don't have 'that sort of thing' in mind."

Rufus was silent.

"We have somebody in mind to whom the approach would be different. We figure there's a fair chance of success. The downside risk—public knowledge of the abduction of a Soviet official in an allied country by an official agency of the United States—is quite simply unacceptable. So the plan you work out, Rufus, would have to provide bulletproof protection against that exposure. You're smarter than anyone at *that* sort of thing, so I didn't come here with a plan that goes beyond one central point."

Rufus looked at him, said nothing.

But now Serge spoke.

"I do not understand. I do not mean that I do not understand the importance of the mission, I do understand the importance of the mission. And it is true I am a physicist by profession. But how can I possibly—no, no," he shook his head, "it is impossible, impossible. Me! I know those people. I go to school with those people. They know me. They will recognize me even now. For them I am the traitor. No, it is quite impossible. Who are you going to . . . kidnap? Blagonravov? You will perhaps be thinking next you will be getting state secrets from Lenin! Poloskov? He puts his mouth on Stalin's behind twenty times twenty times twenty times twenty years—but if you want me to go to the France to give Poloskov a feeling for my fists, I will go. Mirtov? Mirtov knows only about the speed of light and the frequency of the orgasms. No, my dear Director, I would like to help . . ."

"I had none of these men in mind."

"Then who?"

"Viktor Kapitsa."

Serge shot up, turning his chair over. His face had turned white, and the words were whispered.

"Viktor . . . They are permitting *Viktor* to go with the delegation to Paris? No, no—*Viktor Kapitsa in Paris?*"

"His name has been filed with the French authorities as a member of the delegation."

"I was eight years with Viktor in Vorkuta." Serge spoke the words as if at a morgue.

"I know that," the Director answered.

Jerry came in and said dinner was ready. "If that's what you want to call it" he added chirpily as, imitating the gesture of a maître d'hôtel, he bowed low, indicating with exaggerated motion the direction of the dining room.

Chapter 5

VADIM PLATOV wondered why, on that day, the train had moved only for a half hour. But then he also wondered why he continued to spend time wondering about anything, let alone evidence of logistical irrationality. The reason—he concluded—was that his mind continued to work. How long would *that* go on? He had been given a tenner under Article 56, Section 10, which was directed at nonspecified forms of "Anti-Soviet Agitation." Instantly his mind had gone to work to collate the random statistics he had begun idly assembling when, two years earlier, Stalin had reintroduced the draconian *katorga*. Would he *live* ten years?—under the conditions in Vorkuta? As a scientist, he warned himself sternly, he had to deal scientifically with scientific evidence: It never pays, in science, to deceive oneself. "What is the point in building a bridge which will fall down?" the professor at the engineering school at Kiev had once observed.

Not that Vadim Platov had ever been interested in building bridges, but he was very much interested in the scientific principles involved in bridge building. It was in physics, not engineering, that he had distinguished himself, graduating with honors in the class of 1938 and winning a fellowship to study under Academician Pekrovskii, the astrophysicist. He wished instead that he had devoted all those thousands of hours to the study of hypnotism. He couldn't quite remember whether hypnotists could hypnotize themselves—or just other people . . . Perhaps, he ruminated, he might have succeeded in hypnotizing himself by looking at a mirror and practicing on himself the same skills he practiced on others. Then, then, after hard concentration—he might succeed in causing himself to lose consciousness. Consciousness of the cold. In about a half hour it would be his turn to lie on the floor, and the turn of his two companions to sit on him, one on the legs, the other on the torso, thus providing him a little extra warmth. In approximately a half hour Glinka—the illiterate Glinka, little Glinka with the eye patch, the two missing front teeth, and the perpetual smile—Glinka would advise them that a half hour had gone by, because of course their watches, those of them who had watches—Vadim had had a watch, won it as a prize after his paper was published—had been taken from them at the processing center at Riga, but one of the men, the big Kurd, had hidden his. A clumsy guard had forgotten to make him open his mouth. Glinka told the men that all his life he had had the gift of time, that he never used a watch nor needed the summons of a bell but would come in from the fields to receive his lunch and his supper at exactly the specified hour even as a young boy, and his parents, who had a radio, would show him off to their family and friends, saying, "Tell us when it will be six o'clock, Glinka." In due course he would raise his little hand and say in a high happy voice, "It is nearing six o'clock, Father." Whereupon the father would turn up the volume and, inevitably, within a moment or two, Radio Moscow would announce that the hour was six o'clock.

They had found the man who had hidden his watch. And soon after that the Armenian began smoking cigarettes which he had now mysteriously come by, and the big bearded Kurd whose watch had been discovered and who had been beaten for concealing it observed the Armenian with ill-disguised suspicion. Shortly after Glinka called out the hour of midnight, the sixty occupants of the railway car heard a stifled cry followed by a gurgle followed by silence, and the next day when the door was opened and the five pails of gruel were slid into the car, the prisoner nearest the door jerked his thumb behind his shoulder and said, "The Armenian is dead." From behind him the prisoners passed up the corpse and flung it over the side. The guard called for an officer from the command car. A captain came, looked at the corpse, and up again at the impassive faces he could see framed by the space opened up by the door. He hesitated, whispered instructions to an orderly, then removed a whistle from deep inside his vest and blew three times on it. In a few seconds six guards with semiautomatic AK-47s stood behind him at attention. The officer looked up at the men huddled about the railway car opening.

"Tonight," he called out in a rasping voice, creating clouds of steam in the subzero cold, "you will not get your rations." The prisoners were silent.

"And right now," the officer's voice achieved a mechanical stridency, "we shall teach you that executions are a privilege of the Soviet State, not of counterrevolutionaries."

The orderly returned with a sheet of paper. The officer looked at it, turning it around so that the typed roster faced his orderly, to whom he said in a loud voice: "Place your finger on one number." The orderly did so.

"Call out that number."

"V 282."

"V 282, present yourself."

There was no motion from within the car.

"For every minute I am kept waiting, I shall add another number." The silence, thought Vadim, whose own number was V 280, was profounder than any he had ever heard, profounder even than the silence when the colonel had risen to pronounce sentence on him at Riga.

In exactly one minute, the captain repeated the ritual with the orderly, who now called out, "Number V 295!"

At this point there was a shout from the end of the car, and the men moved to permit the Kurd passage to the open door. He looked down at the officer, spat, and said: "Let them alone. It was me." With dignity he managed to lower himself to the siding. The officer pointed to a telephone pole ten meters away and the Kurd was led there. His hands were tied behind the pole and, immobilized, he faced his comrades. Three of the six soldiers, on command, hoisted their rifles and fired. The officer withdrew his pistol from its holster, approached the Kurd, slumped now over to one side, and shot him behind the head. Vadim looked across the width of the car at the young man of his own age who had not uttered a word in the three weeks since their common journey began. His hair was blond, and a bandage of sorts was wound about his left ear. His eyes were streaming tears.

On noticing that Vadim was staring at him, Viktor Kapitsa turned his face away, but in that railway car there was no privacy, and Vadim Platov knew that although he had not studied hypnotism, or extrasensory perception, he had succeeded in communicating to the young man that he, Vadim, was forever grateful to him for this comment of tears. Vadim himself closed his eyes, and suddenly the words appeared before him which he had not thought to utter since he was twelve years old and his grandmother died, thereby relieving him of the (counterrevolutionary) task of a daily recitation. He prayed: He prayed for the Kurd, prayed for the stranger across the way, prayed for the executioners, prayed for Stalin—but his scientific training then asserted itself. If he prayed for Stalin—prayed that Stalin should mend his ways—then Stalin might become commendable, and if he was commendable, Vadim would logically be obliged to revere him. But all he could ever do was hate the monster, so he must *not* pray for him, otherwise he would face a terrible dilemma. He remembered suddenly that his grandmother, who had actually traveled abroad before the Revolution and studied philosophy in Germany as a girl, once told him that not even God could ordain a contradiction. He was very hungry. But the five pails of gruel with the long-handled spoons sat there in the silence, untouched. The guard, looking briefly over his shoulder in the direction of the officers' car, slid the door shut without removing the pails, as he would normally have done. The door would not open again until the next morning; captain's orders.

* * *

It was, Vadim reckoned, the warmest day of the summer. The temperature was above freezing and, at midday, he even found himself unbuttoning his heavy jacket, experiencing a sensual thrill felt not more than a dozen days in the year. He sat with his back to the great pile of frozen wooden railroad ties—the weather would never be warm for long enough to thaw them out, and in his gloved hand he fondled the eleven-ounce lump of bread which was the whole of the day's hard rations: At the end of the day they would be given a pint of a fishy gruel, and, at breakfast time, nothing. Vadim said to his companion, "Viktor, today I think, I think that we are going to make it."

Viktor Kapitsa had begun to chew on his bread. He ate very slowly, with deliberation, and did not speak while he chewed. "I don't know, Vadim. We have five more years. Shall we play again at our game?"

Statistics, with improvisations on numbers and concepts, was their principal diversion. Viktor had been what they called a "calculating prodigy." At age five he could give out the sum of a list of figures, each with as many as four digits, of whatever length. His father felt it his duty to report this peculiarity to the party secretary at the 8th District of Kharkov where Viktor's father worked as bookkeeper at the shoe factory that was the center of commercial life in the 8th District. The secretary was held in awe because he had been present (he was a railroad porter) at the Finland Station when Lenin arrived there on that great day in April. Vitkovsky amused himself for a half hour interrogating the little boy and giving him longer and longer lists to add. The boy's little voice without hesitation gave the answer to the first question: How much is 578 plus 624 plus 1009 plus 333? The secretary painfully added the figures to corroborate the boy's accuracy. After the next question, he stopped, confident that Viktor was giving the correct reply. He tried then the multiplication tables. "How much is 381 times 411?" On these Viktor would hesitate, closing his eyes and shaking his hair slightly, but the delay was never more than for a second or two. There were conferences, and it was decided that when he became seven years old, the state should take Viktor to a special school in Moscow where he would keep company with the brightest young sons of Lenin's associates and develop his skill in such a way as to be of maximum use to the state. The elder Kapitsa felt free to urge on the secretary the comparative advantages of keeping the boy in Kharkov, but the secretary by this time spoke as though it had been the personal decision of Lenin himself that Viktor should go away to school. Happily, Lenin died before Viktor was seven and the secretary disappeared without a trace, leaving his successor with no known file on Viktor Kapitsa, who, accordingly, went to the regular Soviet school. There his precocity was acknowledged enthusiastically by a stocky, imperious woman in her sixties who had taught the children since before the inauguration of the last Czar. She took over Viktor's schooling, and arranged that at age thirteen he should indeed go away—to a special school, fashioned after the German *gymnasia,* where Viktor was introduced to physics. His avid pursuit of it carried him through the university at Kharkov and then to the Lenin Institute for graduate work and, finally, experimental work under Perelman and Fortikov, disciples of the great Tsiolkovskii, who had founded GIRD—in Russian, the Group for the Study of Reactive Motion. By the mid-thirties GIRD had evolved into a rocket research program where, at age twenty-one, Viktor Kapitsa, fair, lithe, even-featured, slightly distracted in demeanor, was acknowledged as a young man of established achievement, having already published an astonishing paper on the aerodynamic problems of space flight which was distributed among laboratory technicians of the Moscow Military Air Academy.

"Ah, Viktor," Vadim now replied, "in your company, of what help can I be to you with statistics? Besides, are we not equipped to deal with measured competence with respect to the variables? It is not likelier ever to be colder than it was during Christmas week of 1948. They have not increased our rations since the day we arrived here. We have managed, between us, to steal an average of 280 ounces of bread per month. Your special relationship with our dear captain's wife, whose quarters you scrub, has netted us an average of twenty-four ounces of cod-liver oil per month. I don't know what I weigh, but I don't think I weigh one ounce less than I weighed one month after we got here. Looking at you, my dear Viktor, is a singularly unpleasant experience: Your skin is yellow, your lips are blue, your face is freckled with frostbite scars, your blond stubble is uneven—it is fortunate I don't have to look at your face except at night" (both men wore balaclavas the bottom part of which they moved up to nose level when they ate), "but you do not look worse than you did soon after we got here. We have put in our twelve hours a day seven days a week and neither of us has had dysentery in over a year. What have you got to say to that?"

Viktor pointed to the horizon on the left, where the wooden profile of Vorkuta's barracks could be seen and, one hundred meters to the right, a mound, taller than the tallest building, and stretching a kilometer off to the right like a huge ice dirigible beached in the snow.

"That," said Viktor, pointing to the corpses of ten thousand men who had passed through Vorkuta, "is my answer."

"Ah," said Vadim, who felt today a strange elation, "but look at this, my doubting Thomas," and he raised his hand. "That is not the hand of a corpse. That is the hand of Vadim Platov." He lowered his hand. "And who decided that I should lower my arm? The Gulag Archipelago? Captain Popolov? The Great Shithead in the Kremlin? No, it is Vadim Platov who decided just now to lower his arm. And listen, listen carefully"—the nearest guard was nowhere within hearing distance, but Vadim lowered his voice theatrically—"listen: 'Our Father, Who art in heaven, hallowed be Thy name. . . .' Nothing that they have done to us has kept me from remembering those words, and I know that they mean more than"—by instinct, he turned his head to one side—"than everything ever written by Marx and Lenin."

Viktor's teeth flashed into a smile, and he ripped off his balaclava, and the lines of an old man's face were visible, corrugating the sunken cheeks, but the eyes were young. "Ah, Vadim, how would I have survived except for you! My beloved Vadim, you know nothing about fate, or historical necessity. You don't allow yourself to remember now, with a few ounces of bread in your stomach, that you will wake at midnight from the cold and from the awful pain from your parched stomach. They will call us out, as usual, sometime between twelve and two, for a roster-check, and you will experience, for the thousandth time, a little fire of indignation. And you will return to the bunk and spend half an hour trying to contrive your body and the rags we have collected over five years into a position so as to make sleep possible. And then both of us, I know, will play mentally with figures, and our theories of spaces, trying to think, think of something except that we have lived a lifetime, every night is a lifetime, every night we have no reason to expect that our lives, our bodies, can accept one more day of . . . this. But now you speak as if you were lying at a beach on the Black Sea wondering whether you would go to the smorgasbord before, or after, lying with your girl friend. . . . Vadim—"

The whistle blew. The conversation stopped in midsentence. All over the area men rose—220, in this detachment—and lifted their picks, their shovels, the ties, the wheelbarrows with the rock and gravel, and at that slow, deliberate pace from which no prisoner ever varied, they went back to the railroad bed to work a second six hours, during which no conversation was permitted except to ask questions of a supervisor. A cloud suddenly occluded the sun, which was not seen again on that day in July.

* * *

At five-thirty on that memorable morning the following March the great bell did not sound. By habit, most of the prisoners in Detachment D woke anyway. There were no watches, so that nobody could say with certainty that the hour was past when the guard would unlock the door and shout out to the men to move outside to relieve themselves in the open latrine before lining up in the dark to march out to the work area. But an hour went by, and through the crack in the door a prisoner announced that he could see traces of light, and the word spread through the barrack to the two hundred men who lay in their bunks dressed in exactly the same clothes they would wear marching out the door to work, the temperature inside the barrack being forty-five degrees. Something was up.

Vadim whispered to Viktor. "Perhaps there is another hunger strike?" The reference was to the strike in 1949 in Detachment L. The spokesman for the men had announced, when the guard opened the door in the morning, that the detachment would not go out to work without receiving food. The demand was for five ounces of bread in the morning. The other detachments were kept locked throughout the day, eighty thousand prisoners ignorant of the ongoing drama.

It was not until that evening that the routine was resumed, and although the barracks' doors had opened only to admit the kitchen zeks with the great cans of gruel, and they—supervised, as ever, by two armed guards—said nothing, everyone suddenly knew; in the way that, in a prison, everyone knows when a prisoner has been executed.

The hunger strikers had been told in midafternoon that their request was granted. Joyfully they had filed out toward the work area, two kilometers distant, where they had been told the baker's truck awaited them. Exercising caution, the prisoners' spokesman specified that the ration would have to include the normal midday ration of twelve ounces *in addition to* the five ounces bargained for during the morning, and the commandant said that he understood the terms well. The men marched toward food, their spirits exuberant by this unheard-of victory. As they marched forward toward the railroad bed the guards, normally abreast of the detachment, began casually to fall behind until there were, in fact, only the two columns of prisoners. It was then, from hastily improvised foxholes in the snow, that the machine gunners went to work. There were of course no survivors, and the commandant had issued crisp orders that the corpses would remain where they had fallen, as monuments to the incivility of the criminal class and the expeditiousness of Soviet justice. That was four years ago, and although the population of Vorkuta was constantly refreshed, there were still enough old-timers to ensure the unlikelihood that another detachment would attempt a hunger strike. "It has got to be something else," said Viktor.

It was noon before the guards opened the door and called out the men. Vadim squinted, the sight being unusual. It was dark when the men rose to go to work, dark when they returned—only during the summer was it still light. So it had been seven months since Vadim had seen the endless files of scruffy men, as far as the eye could see, in double ranks, shuffling their arms and feet to gain protection against the zero temperature. No noise was tolerated, not even the clapping of gloved hands—in order that the commands of the detachment captains might be heard clearly. But today they heard the rasp of the amplifiers, posted on high telephone poles at intervals of about fifty meters in all directions. These were infrequently used, but were the instrument by which the commandant occasionally addressed the entire population of this island of the Archipelago.

"Prisoners of the Soviet State! Hear this! Silence! Hear this! Yesterday, the great father of our beloved socialist republic passed away. I know that your grief will incapacitate you"

—*"that sadist is incapable of sarcasm,"* thought Vadim, his heart pounding with joy—

"so that in memory of our beloved Marshal Stalin, we shall suspend the work requirement for the balance of the day so that you can mourn his passing. You will all return to your barracks."

And here—never mind that the noise would be overheard—there was no restraint. Men who had not smiled in years broke out with laughter that became nearly hysterical. Men who had not spoken to each other embraced. They shouted and they sang in uninhibited dissonance, each man yelling out whatever hymn of thanksgiving occurred to him. The jubilation would have gone on into the night except that the biological instinct so highly developed in survival circumstances—to husband one's energies—gradually asserted itself, and the men fell gradually into a kind of comatose silence. But Vadim and Viktor, sitting on the lower bunk, talked on excitedly. Vadim whispered that surely the death of the monster would affect their prison terms? Playfully he asked Viktor: "It is

2,928 days since I was sentenced. What percentage of my tenner have I done?" Viktor closed his eyes, grinned, and asked: "To how many decimal places do you want your answer?"

"Four!" Vadim answered coquettishly.

"80.0022 percent," said Viktor.

"Well, don't you think our new masters might consider remitting the . . . 19.9978 we have left over?"

"No," said Viktor. "Probably they have forgotten we exist."

It was several months before the folkways of Archipelago began gradually to change. The first sign was the commandant's advising the men that they would each be permitted to write one letter, on not more than two sides of a sheet of paper, which, together with one pencil, would be issued the following day. The rations were increased by four ounces with very nearly miraculous physical effect, Viktor and Vadim agreed, most noticeably permitting sounder sleep. It required a huge act of will, but both men regularly husbanded one third of their noonday ration, and ate it the following morning. They noticed before many weeks had gone by that the ranks of Vorkuta were diminishing without any significant bloating of the ice dirigible. Still, in their own detachment, though six men had died in July and there were no replacements, no one was called to the processing center, the staging area for torture, execution—and release.

But the day came. Viktor and Vadim had not dared to give voice to that which both feared most: that one should be released while the other stayed. The prospect of one day in the Archipelago without each other was a thought neither could permit himself to express. They were both, in fact, summoned from their work area one Wednesday in August and led by a guard to the processing center, where they were directed to a cubicle in one of the administrative buildings. Pictures on the wall were of Khrushchev and Bulganin, and the bulletin board was thick with communications from that huge spectral building in Moscow, the ganglion of the Archipelago. Viktor was called in first and told to sit down on the stool opposite the clerk, who was dressed in a shapeless brown corduroy and wore a heavy vest and rimless glasses and a trim moustache. He studied the papers on the unpainted table.

"Kapitsa. Yes, anti-Soviet agitation . . . protested deportation of traitors on eastern front in a letter to the rector of the University of Kharkov. Hm. Well, Kapitsa, the Soviet State, exercising its customary mercy, has granted you an amnesty. Moreover, the Moscow Military Air Academy has . . . requested . . . that you report for duty there. Within thirty days. You are to go to General Bolknovitinov. Do you agree? Sign here." Viktor Kapitsa, his hand shaking, took the pen and signed his name on the form without bothering to read it. He was given a release order, a train pass to Kharkov, and ten rubles. Vadim Platov was dealt with similarly, and told to report to an institute in Kiev whose name he did not recognize. He was emboldened to ask what it was that was needed of him. "The state requires the services of all its trained scientists." When could they leave? The clerk looked at his watch. It was eleven. "There is a train at one o'clock. You change at Ust for Moscow."

One o'clock! The station was a mere one-kilometer distant. Clutching his release papers, Vadim left the cubicle for the anteroom, where Viktor was waiting for him. They did not speak, could not speak, but walked silently to their empty barrack. To put together their belongings was the work of five minutes. They must not misgauge the time, but the bell at noon summoning the camp personnel to lunch would give them exactly one hour's advance notice of the train's departure. Feverishly they set about writing, with the stubby pencils they now possessed, notes of farewell to their companions, having agreed to write joint notes so as to cover as many as possible. They reckoned what they supposed must be half an hour after the bell. They had written a total of forty notes, which they distributed on the frayed canvas bunks of the addressees. They picked up their satchels and went out the door at the usual pace and turned, this time not east toward the endless railroad line but west toward the building from which smoke always rose, in the direction of their youth. They could see the outlines of a dozen railroad cars. Simultaneously both men began to walk at a brisk pace unexperienced in years. Their bearing was now erect. Viktor with his topcoat of sorts, sewn together from three separate remnants of jacket material, and the shawl wound about his head and ears, Vadim with the heavy jacket, a coarse piece of string girding it tightly about his fleshless waist, patched trousers, heavy shoes much dilapidated. Suddenly Viktor paused, laid down his satchel, and ceremoniously removed his balaclava; Vadim did the same. Cautiously they inserted these lifesaving face masks in their satchels, and resumed their march. At the gate, so ferociously guarded with high turrets, machine guns, and dogs, their documents were accepted routinely and, giddy with the sensation, they walked out of Gulag and climbed the staircase to the station level unsurveilled, for the first time in eight years, by armed guards. Inside, a sergeant at the ticket window inspected their travel passes and issued them a stub for the journey to Ust. Was the train leaving on time? Vadim asked, as if he were a boulevardier asking a routine question at the Gare du Nord. The clerk stared at him incredulously, uttered a profanity, and returned to his chair by the stove. Vadim looked at Viktor, who said, "There's the train. Why not board it?" Intoxicated by their authority over their own movements, they moved up the steps of the car, half expecting that at any moment they would be recalled. Timidly Vadim opened the carriage door and was overcome by the heat within. He had not experienced such comfort since leaving the courthouse where he was sentenced. Two dozen men, half of them prison personnel on leave, half of them liberated prisoners from other detachments, were sitting on the wooden slatted benches *with backrests*. Vadim and Viktor sat opposite each other, lowering themselves carefully onto the unaccustomed chairs. A guard approached them. He bore a large heavy covered tray at waist level, strapped behind his neck.

"You have money?"

They nodded. He uncovered the tray and they saw rolls, sausage, cheese; enough, Vadim thought, to bring the whole of their detachment to delirium.

"How much?" He struggled for urbanity.

Five kopecks bought them each as much as they could eat. That was not a great deal, because their stomachs rebelled at such unaccustomed richness. They finished just as the train began to move. They looked out the window. The sky was a curdled yellow, the ground specked by snow, the squat barracks gray and frostbitten and bleak. The ice dirigible had assumed a perfect symmetry.

Viktor looked at Vadim and said, "You were right, Vadim." Vadim looked up curiously, as if to say: Right about what? "You were right," Viktor repeated. "We did survive. But I would not be here except for you," and the tears came down again, and Vadim thought back on the boyish face of that very young man, in the other railway car, with the tears, which would take a lifetime to dry.

Chapter 6

BLACKFORD OAKES ordered a second coffee and the bill in French that obviously suffered from underutilization compounding undercultivation. He tilted back his chair and smiled. He recalled Sally's crestfallen self-esteem at this same outdoor café when, four years ago, they had vacationed together. She had been studying French intensively for her orals and was protective of her lover's manifest disability. It was their first lunch in Paris. Looking at the menu he told her he would take the *escalope de veau*. She said that she, not being hungry, would merely have a ham sandwich. She relayed his order to the waiter with aplomb but when she came around to her own, visible distress set in and Blackford suddenly heard her order *"Deux sandwiches de jambon."*

"I thought you weren't hungry?" he commented as the waiter walked off.

"I'm not," she snapped, arching her eyebrows in what he had come to know as her defensive look. "I couldn't remember whether *a* sandwich is masculine or feminine. . . ." Then she smiled. "When you get a little older, Blacky, and have a little more experience," she said, mocking at once his French and his style, "you too will develop a little *savoir-faire* and syntactical ingenuity."

How much he missed her, he thought as he glanced yet again at his watch, balancing the newspaper on his lap; and then reproached himself for missing anybody, or anything, on such a day as this in Paris in June. It was the kind of day Hollywood producers . . . produce, in order to star Audrey Hepburn in a poignant romance. The sky was just *that* shade of blue, the temperature warm but with that vernal energy of late spring. The wind played lackadaisically with the leaves on the trees that lined the ancient, lively street. He decided to walk and therefore set out earlier than he had planned. He paid the bill, left the change, and returned the waitress's smile: They all smiled at Blackford, in part because of his inviting informality of manner, in part because he seemed to so many women so endearingly at ease in every situation; but mostly, Sally had told him—amused, he remembered her words—"because you are disgustingly handsome, lover boy. It's a pity under the circumstances that all you know is how to build bridges and kill people." That was her technique for getting him heatedly to deny that he was in fact engaged professionally in the business of "killing people," which indeed he was not in the business of doing. But he knew that any denial was a step in the direction of isolating the truth: like Twenty Questions. So he had replied mock-solemnly, "If you're as good-looking as I am, people don't mind being killed by you—it's just that simple. The CIA thinks of everything." He remembered her at the airport yesterday, the wind blowing her light brown hair across her forced smile, dressed in the green blouse and the white cotton skirt, with tiny pearl earrings, and somehow looking like freshly poured champagne. He put away any further consideration of the dilemma she had left him with, folded the newspaper in hand, and began to walk.

As a matter of routine now he walked alert, taking unobtrusive opportunities to try to ascertain whether he was being followed. He had been absolutely certain, in Budapest in October, that he had not been followed; and yet . . . He turned left at Rivoli, and right to traverse the Ile de la Cité, crossing between Notre Dame and the Palais de Justice on over the Pont St.-Michel, where he half expected to trip over Jean Dufy, whose favorite bridge it obviously was, and with good reason. As he walked up Boulevard St.-Michel through the university section and past the Luxembourg Gardens he gave thought, having read the paper, to the mind-boggling incapacity of Frenchmen to govern themselves, and then checked himself to examine whether he harbored any latent bias against the French, decided that in fact he did not, and therefore reregistered his dismay over the mind-boggling incapacity of Frenchmen to govern themselves. The incumbent—he had seen the figures in a profile in *Le Monde*—was the twenty-fourth Prime Minister since the war, and everyone was giving odds he wouldn't last through the summer. They were hopping mad, the politicians in the paper this morning, at Senator John Kennedy's having given a speech yesterday defending independence for Algeria. "Senator Kennedy," one politician had declaimed on the floor of the Assembly, "will be recalled by those Frenchmen with mischievous memories as the son of the ambassador to Great Britain whose principal contribution to international diplomacy was to inform President Roosevelt, while serving him as ambassador to the Court of St. James in 1940, that the Nazis would surely win the war and that under the circumstances there was no point whatever in any intervention by the United States. The son clearly inherits his father's political acuity." Hm. He might—Blackford mused as he shortened his pace to prolong his exposure to smells that billowed out from the bakery he was passing—at least have gone on to mention that the young Kennedy had fought in the Pacific, where he either got rammed by a PT boat, or rammed a PT boat, whichever is better; and apparently had behaved with commendable courage. Besides—Blackford's polemical energies were rising in reaction to a manifestly anti-American challenge—what Frenchman is in a position to reproach anybody, anywhere, on the subject of diplomacy? Here they were, stuck in Algeria—after being defeated in Indochina—after being defeated by the Germans—one generation after they'd have been defeated by the Germans save for the intervention of Mr. Wilson, two generations after losing to the Germans in 1870. Sheeyit. Lecturing us on foreign policy! He recalled the indignation of Eddie Condon at their last lapse into advice. "Do we tell the frogs how to jump on grapes?"

As he turned left on Port Royal, he instinctively looked to his left. He had developed, in six years with the Company, a fairly reliable capacity for detecting any unnatural synchronization of movement. A half-dozen times, in as many years, he had spotted it as clearly as, looking down on a stroboscope placed on a turntable, the eye would detect a clockwise or counterclockwise deviation, alerting you to whether the turntable speed was off-kilter. He noticed no one, but instead of staying on the side of the street where, one half block down, he would meet the man, he crossed it, and turned the corner of the little side street opposite. There he waited, as if examining the names on the doorway of the apartment building. Nobody went by; so, checking his watch, which read one minute past three, he crossed back over the street, into the doorway at No. 128, took out a key from his pocket, climbed one set of stairs, and used the same key to open the door to the first-floor apartment, tapping the doorbell lightly even as he opened the door. A voice from within a room beyond the narrow hallway said, "Come in, Blackford."

Blackford knew in what situation he would probably find him: sitting in an armchair, behind a coffee table on which would be papers with markings on them no one but their author could hope to understand. Rufus would be slightly pale, slightly heavy, slightly formal, and—he supposed, several years having gone by—slightly older.

It was as he expected, in a comfortable old room with high ceilings and ceiling-high door-windows, a large comfortable living room, with even a little color, mostly from those artful gallery posters the French like so much to buy and frame. There were chairs and sofas enough for a dozen people.

"Well, Rufus," said Blackford, extending his hand, "I see Mammon is looking after you. You'd have to pay fifty bucks a day for this at the Ritz."

Rufus's efforts at small talk were undistinguished.

"I am glad to see you again, Blackford. I understand you have been busy."

"Yeah. I helped lose Hungary, though—that was too bad."

Rufus had experienced that tone of voice on another occasion, and changed tack. He rose and walked into the kitchen. "Coffee?"

"Thanks. Assassination?"

"No," came the steady voice from the kitchen.

"Torture?"

"No."

"Kidnapping?"

"Yes."

Blackford yawned. "Well, I'm glad I didn't come all the way to

Paris just to . . ." he paused: *Rufus really didn't like obscenity—* "muck about."

He walked into the kitchen to give Rufus a hand.

* * *

It was nearly dark outside when Rufus was done briefing him. As was his habit, he suggested to Blackford that he put off any pursuit of the finer points of the plan until after he had had an opportunity to digest what he had been told. "It might even be better if we talked again only after you have met 'Serge' "—he consciously pseudonymized the name—"and see Trust. They're both at St.-Firmin now, and you have your choice of going over there later on tonight or tomorrow morning. The telephone number"— he slowed his pace of talking and accentuated his syllables, which was a clue to Blackford that he was expected to memorize the number—"is . . . 682-583. You are to ask for 'Mr. Tuck' and announce yourself as 'Julian Booth.' What do you say?"

Blackford glanced at his watch. It was after seven and he felt restless; and besides, the prospect of seeing Anthony Trust again cheered him. "I've been to Chantilly. I ought to be able to find the Château St.-Firmin without any problem. What about a car?"

Rufus opened a drawer and gave him a key and a garage slip. "Give this to the doorman at your hotel and he'll pull up with a gray Citroën. The registration papers are in the car. An American friend of yours. Had to go back to the States suddenly, lent you the car. You plan to ship it to the States when you're through visiting in France."

They made arrangements for the next meeting, and Blackford walked out of the apartment. Routinely he opened the front door a fraction, peered through the crack as best he could, and stepped out, battered newspaper in hand, and a block down the street hailed a taxi.

Before packing an overnight bag he placed the call. The operator presently rang back. *"Monsieur Tuck sur la ligne."*

"This is Julian Booth. I thought I'd come around now, save time. Is it too late for dinner?"

"Not at all!" The reassuring voice of his old friend had not changed. "We'll expect you . . . ?"

"Figure about nine."

He studied the map in the car intensively and put it away. He would not need to look at it twice; and an hour later, passing by the park at Chantilly, he drove past those famous benches where, during World War I, the generals would pause after lunch during their afternoon promenade to consider strategy. Blackford assumed, judging from the historical results, that the plan likeliest to kill the largest number of Frenchmen was regularly the plan that most commended itself to the chiefs of staff. He turned, drove through the forest, and then took the right lane, over a bridge, past a hedgerow, through an open gate, and up a private drive to a building whose outline he could not easily make out. But the half moon played over a small lake at the bottom of a large lawn, and as he rang the bell, suitcase in hand, the silhouette of the building crystallized in the moon's wake, and he guessed the chateau to have about twenty rooms. Trust, dark, lithe, a year older—his oldest friend—opened the door, and they exchanged handshakes, quickly closing the door. Trust whispered, "We'll have to have our private reunion later. Our friend is sitting in there, and it's getting late for dinner." He led Oakes into the room where the stocky crew-cut Russian with the weathered tan face and corrugated eyelids rose and extended his hand. "They call me Serge."

"They call me Julian."

The maid entered and announced dinner. Trust nodded, and said to Blackford, "She doesn't speak any English and in any case she's cleared. We can speak."

* * *

"Tell me, Serge," Blackford asked as he trimmed off a bit of cheese from the plate and applied it to his bread. "When last did you hear from Kapitsa?"

"I have not heard from my Viktor ever since I saw him in Moscow. I see him on New Year's Eve of 1954. We promised, when the train from Vorkuta came to Moscow and he went to Kharkov, and I to Kiev, that no matter nobody, we would spend New Year's Eve together. And, of course, we wrote letters to each other every week during the in-between, sometimes two, three times every week. Of course we were very careful in our letters. Not Viktor, not I, made any points at all about the authorities. We talked about our work—and even about these matters we were oh so very very careful, because we both are in highly secret work. (I burned in the fireplace every one of his letters before I left for Vienna.) When I saw him, on New Year's Eve, I say to myself, 'Vadim' "— Blackford and Anthony now knew the real name of Serge, and their eyes met over the indiscretion—" 'you will wait for a few hours before you decide if to tell Viktor your plans.' You see, I have decided to defect. I wanted to know if Viktor was in the same mood. If he said yes, then I would have waited, if necessary for one, two, three years, to arrange that we should go together. But the official order to go to Vienna to take the six-week course with Dr. Kuehnelt-Leddihn on the telemetry gave me the opportunity I did not want to pass by."

"What was Kapitsa's mood when you saw him?"

"You wouldn't believe. We met together at six, at a friend's apartment, then to a restaurant together, then walking over Moscow. He took me finally to the train. We talked, yes, about Vorkuta. And, yes, we talked about his work, his *huge* fascination with the physics of rocketry. But what he talked about most, what he talked about ninety percent of the time, was Tamara."

"Tamara?" Blackford asked.

"Tamara—I can remember Viktor's words—I have a good memory, you know, Julian—Tamara is 'more beautiful than Juliet, more learned than Madame Curie, more gentle than the River Don'!"

"Yes, but can she dance?"

"What?" said Vadim.

"She sounds okay," said Oakes.

"Okay! Viktor proves himself *mad, crazy* about his Tamara. He says to me, stopping right there, in the middle of Red Square, he says, 'Look at me, Vadim' "—"Serge" himself recognized this breach of security procedures. He began again. "He said, 'Look at me . . . Am I disgusting to a beautiful twenty-three-year-old girl?' I took my beloved Viktor in my arms, and I say to him, 'Viktor, you are thirty-six years old. Six months ago you looked like a corpse. Today you do not look thirty-six, that is true. But you have color in the cheeks. You have gained ten? fifteen? kilos. You are wise, you are brilliant, you are one of the *finest* men God *ever* made. If you want Tamara, she will be lucky to have you!' Viktor was overjoyed, he was so happy—I could not even begin to tell Viktor what was my intention. But—we walked past Lenin's Tomb, talking, and suddenly he winks at me and he turns most solemnly"—Vadim made the low bow of the Russian peasant—"toward the tomb, put me in front of him so no one can see, and does *this* with his middle finger." Vadim executed the internationally recognized fico. "I whisper to him, 'Do it once more for me,' and he did—but that was the entire whole of the political conversation. If I told him I was intending to leave Russia it would only have done something greatly to hurt his happiness. Because he could not leave Tamara."

"What does she do?" Trust asked.

"She was then a technical assistant. She too is a physicist."

"And that was your last communication?"

Vadim, well into his second brandy, was well into prolixity. It transpired that, as prisoners, he and Viktor had developed a highly intricate code based on numerals. They used to practice it, for distraction, hour after endless hour. No such code, of course, is unbreakable, Vadim reminded them. "But I sent a letter on my way out of Vienna, to the apartment of Viktor's friend who let us use it. It was a letter to say thank you, and of idle chatter about what I have seen in Vienna, written on a typewriter. I made the ribbon to stick, and then started pushing different numbers, putting the ribbon on, and off, as if to be fixing the ribbon. Then at the closing of the letter I asked my friend please to pass it along to Viktor. No one yet knew of my defecting. What I typed in our special code was: 'My dear Viktor: I do what I do because I must. I shall not write you in case you suffer more, and do not write to me. Always your devoted . . .'" This time he paused. "I gave my name."

"Did he marry Tamara?" Oakes asked.

Trust broke in. "We've put together"—he took a file from the drawer of an antique buffet and opened it as they walked into the formal living room—"everything we could find, every public reference, every bulletin; we did as much poking about in Moscow as we could. Our guy asked some routine questions here and there, and here it is: They were married in April 1954. Both Tamara and Kapitsa have had three promotions in the last two years. She is now a full-fledged associate at the aerodynamics laboratory, and he is one of its six research directors, working under General Bolknovitinov. The whole thing is under the general supervision of Academician Nesmayanov, then of Korolyov, the General Groves in the situation, who reports to the chiefs of staff and directly to the Kremlin.

"The Kapitsas have an apartment at the Tyura Tam compound. No children. No notoriety of any sort, that we can come up with. And listen—Kapitsa and his wife have already been abroad. Last year, as part of a scientific exchange visit, Viktor went to Rome with a Russian delegation and delivered a lecture. Tamara was with him, and handled the slides during Viktor's lecture. We found out, in Rome, that the group—there were thirty of them—traveled together everywhere, from the conference, to the hotel, to the sight-seeing places, to the restaurants. There were no incidents, no irregularities, nothing."

"And Tamara was with him," Vadim said, as if to himself. "That is bad, that is very bad."

"Why do you say that?" Trust asked.

"Because if Tamara was with Viktor, and both in a foreign country, it would have been good if they went for asylum, political asylum. If they didn't, they were scared. Or"—he looked down—"or they do not want to leave Russia."

Trust got up. "It's late, Serge—what the hell, Vadim. We've got a lot of detail to go over tomorrow. I'm going to go over a few things with . . . Julian, here."

Vadim rose. "I too am tired. But"—he looked mischievously at them—"not so tired as to not to take myself upstairs maybe a little vodka-soda. You wish me to bring you something from the kitchen?"

"No thanks," Blackford volunteered. "Maybe later." Blackford found himself, rather unexpectedly, on his feet. The least he could do, he reasoned, in deference to someone who had spent eight years in Gulag, and emerged spiritually whole, so far as one could judge. And Blackford tended to judge quickly, though his judgments, while always impatient, were not always reliable.

* * *

"I like him," he said simply to Anthony, after Vadim had gone off noisily to bed.

"I like him, too. There's something about him I'd guess Gulag brought out."

"This one's a pisser, isn't it?"

"Yeah, the brass in Washington are entitled to be pretty desperate if they figure the Soviet Union is going to outperform us in space."

"Those goddam Russians," Blackford mused. "Send people off to slave-labor camps and the next day put 'em to work creating a scientific breakthrough. Maybe we ought to tell them we bought the atmosphere from the Indians, and we're sorry, but No Trespassing. . . . You don't suppose, Anthony, the Russians are superior to Americans?"

"No."

"Maybe communism makes sense?"

"Yeah, right: We might ask Rufus to conduct a seminar."

"Did you travel with Vadim?"

"We came separately. We arrived two hours before you did. I've read his security record. Lives absolutely alone, orders everything he can get his hands on in Russian. He had become reclusive at his little farm in New York. Only Kapitsa could have brought him back into action. He's never got over Vorkuta, the guys who grilled him told me, and I think it's clear that's true."

"It's clear all right. So is the fact that we can't let him operate in any undercover situation when the cover is off the brandy." Blackford stood, looking down at his lanky, earnest friend—"Where's my room?"

Chapter 7

THE VOICE from the loudspeaker on the AN-10 announced curtly that during the refueling stop at East Berlin passengers would remain in their seats. Viktor Kapitsa turned to Tamara—they occupied the rearmost seats and no one, in the half-empty airplane, was occupying the seats across the aisle from them—and winked. She returned the wink, lowered her head slightly, and smiled. She wore her hair in a bun, but it flowed back loosely over the sides of her face, so that there was movement, and a ripple of light, in her brown hair whenever she raised or lowered her head. Her smile was both young and wise: and cautious.

There had been just that one night when they discussed such matters as Soviet authoritarianism explicitly. It was after she told him yes, she would marry him; told him she would never have married any other man, if he had not asked her, and he had broken down with the joy that filled him, and they hugged, and walked and walked until the dawn came in that crystal night during the whole of which the snowflakes came down gently as sanctifying grace.

He talked then about Vorkuta. She knew, of course, about his background. But graduates of *katorga* are disinclined to talk about it, except among themselves. Viktor, in several hours, gave her an idea, but found himself incapable of saying it all. She had heard him speak frequently of his best friend, Vadim Platov, and now he reiterated that he owed to Vadim his survival. "I remember after the first week, I made a very conscious decision. That decision was to die. That was when Vadim wrestled with me. He wrestled with me as desperately as if he had come upon me drowning in the middle of a lake and was determined to bring me to the shore alive with him. It wasn't easy to do. During the work hours we were not permitted to talk, except at the fifteen-minute break for lunch. And at night; in whispers, in the barracks. Vadim took me on. He would force me to listen, force me to use my mind, force me to give attention to what he said. He clearly knew he was engaged in therapy, but he never by any word or movement suggested that I was fainthearted, or crippled, or anything but a human being, with a soul, a mind, and a body that could—theoretically—survive. It took a very, very long time. I came out of it in six months, though I was pessimistic even after that, right up until The Death. We used to play with statistics"—arm in arm they crossed the street, on which traffic had all but disappeared. Tamara knew about Viktor's prowess with figures—"and the statistics weren't reassuring. But Vadim had a way of putting it: 'If there is one survivor in one thousand, there is no objective reason why you should not be that survivor. In fact, there are more than one-per-thousand survivors—so there's room for me, too.' I have to confess, Tamara, that if something had happened to Vadim, I am quite certain that I would have edged back to desperation, then lassitude, stupor, death. We saw it happen. Over and over again. They could have worn placards: 'PLEASE DO NOT DISTURB. I AM ENGAGED IN DYING. IT WILL TAKE A WHILE. PARDON THE INCONVENIENCE.'"

He spoke then about his detestation of the system. "Stalin was certainly unique. There cannot have been two Stalins in the history of just one planet. Stalin in a zoo, that would have redeemed the socialist experiment. Stalin as chief of state: that is a condemnation of a system. But I have made up my mind, and you are the principal reason for it. I will never speak about the system. About Soviet politics. Not to anybody. Not"—he gripped her hand—"to you, after tonight. It is the only way. Total abstinence. I am a political celibate, as of this moment and, you will soon discover"—he grinned, and there was, way back there, the trace of the sometime boy—"all my tensions, from the time we marry, will be priapic." Tamara smiled, and rested her head on his shoulder, as he went on talking.

And that was, and remained, the protocol.

But over the next few years, although they never broke the code, it was a part of their intimacy to experience together the frustrations particular to the system, the forms, the interrogations, the inquiries about fellow workers, the obviously intercepted mail, the eavesdropping, the telephone taps. "I have two tasks ahead of me," Viktor had said on that white night as he held her back suddenly to avoid a speeding official car. "The first is to help design a rocket that will reach either the moon or Washington, D.C.; the second is to find an apartment for us. The first is an immensely complex project and will almost certainly prove easier than the second."

* * *

They lingered in East Berlin for very nearly two hours, sitting in the hot airplane, and of course no explanation was given. Finally they were airborne, and beer and cold sandwiches were passed around. Viktor munched on his and said, "I wonder if there will be any deviation from the sort of thing we did in Rome?"

"Not according to the schedule."

Indeed their time was to be taken up from breakfast until their return to the hotel, the Grand. She fished out a sheaf of papers from her purse, and began to read aloud: "Monday. 0730: Convene for breakfast. 0830: Bus departs for Lycée. 0900–1200: Sessions, Lycée. 1210: Depart on bus to hotel. 1300: Lunch. 1400: Return to Lycée by bus. 1430–1700: Lycée. 1700–1830: Bus tour of Paris. 1900: Reception, Soviet Embassy . . . Shall I go on?"

"Do we get to see Versailles?"

She scanned the three sheets of paper.

"No. But we get to see the Museum of the 1870 Commune."

"Louvre?"

"Yes, Wednesday."

"Maybe some evening, after we are taken back to the hotel, we can get out?"

"It says here, 'No member of the delegation shall leave the hotel except as specified in this schedule. Any emergencies should be discussed with Pyotr Viksne.'" Viksne served them now, even as on the trip to Rome, as (a) tour director, (b) political officer, and (c) KGB agent. On the guest list given to the French, he was referred to as "Academician Viksne."

"Perhaps we should call him at two in the morning and tell him the toilet doesn't work?"

"Better not. The plumbers' union in Paris may be a Communist union, and we'd be nailed with an Article 58."

Both of them recognized they were flirting with a transgression of The Protocol. No doubt flying over free territory—they were nearing the Rhine—had made them licentious.

They returned to their reading and, as they crossed Paris on the approach to Orly, craned to view the city they had read about since childhood. Tamara spotted the Eiffel Tower and yelled out her pleasure so loudly that other members of the delegation in turn strained to see out the little cloudy windows of the plane. Ivan Dyakov, with his omnipresent camera, leaned high over Viktor and Tamara to take a picture. At the platform a welcoming committee from the Union of Democratic Scientists met them and there were two or three reporters and photographers. The reporters asked, through interpreters, when the Russians would launch a satellite. Academician Nesmayanov, on behalf of the delegation, smiled, and pulling out a notebook read out in rapid French: *"Nous sommes très heureux de visiter en France pour aider les travaux scientifiques pour la libération du peuples opprimés. Nous seront bien heureux de recevoir, en septembre, les distingués scientistes français pour leur retourner l'hommage qu'ils nous offerent."* He folded the note neatly, put it in his pocket, and proceeded down the corridor followed by his delegation, without any further thought given to the press.

"What did he say?"—Viktor had trouble with French spoken rapidly—he asked Tamara.

"The usual business. Thanked our hosts, said we democratic scientists have a lot in common, and we will be glad to see them in September."

Viktor said nothing. As requested, he handed his own and Tamara's passports to Viksne, who muttered in Russian that he would return them on the plane going back. "You won't need them until then." And there, as always, was the bus, parked only a few paces from the baggage compartment.

Chapter 8

BORIS ANDREYEVICH BOLGIN WAS in Paris on his monthly visit from London and, as ever, occupied the office of the military attaché, who obligingly moved—somewhere; Bolgin did not bother to ask and did not care where. Everybody was obliging to Bolgin, ambassadors included, because Bolgin's dispositions tended to be accepted in Moscow as final. The wonder of it was that he had survived the purge of Beria, notwithstanding Bolgin's high standing as chief of KGB counterintelligence for Western Europe and therefore his presumed closeness to his boss. Twelve long years earlier, when Stalin reinstated the *katorga* and appeared hungry to send there everyone who ever worked for him, Bolgin had reached a calm decision, the fruit of that serenity uniquely disposed of by many who had already experienced *katorga*, as Bolgin had, during a purge in the thirties. He never traveled without his cyanide pill; that was his daytime rule. His nighttime rule: Never go to sleep sober. A corollary of this rule was: Never seek companionship, male or female, at dinner or later. As a younger man he liked to talk, and he liked especially to talk when he was well lubricated. When they let him out of the camp, requiring as they did his language skills in the war, he was a changed man, receiving stoically the news of his wife's divorce and disappearance with their child.

He simply went to work, using his skills as a linguist and his cunning as a spy, and then spymaster. He had made it a rule to resist as forcefully as he could any promotion. In that way he never troubled his superiors or his peers. He pleaded with Ilyich not to give him all of Western Europe. But Ilyich had insisted, and Bolgin reluctantly accepted the assignment, on the understanding that all disciplinary arrangements would be made by Moscow, directly. In that way he survived, combining an apparent fair-mindedness with absolute personal privacy and that mysteriousness that came from nobody's knowing, as ambassadors and agents came and went, whether they had been summoned to Moscow, for reward or for punishment, as the result of one of Boris Andreyevich Bolgin's personal communications.

He was one of six Soviet agents in Europe who had the privilege of a personal code. When he elected to use that code, which was frequently, he would eject the operator from the encoding room and tap out his message himself. He would be brought replies, or instructions, from Moscow in the same code, undecipherable except by himself.

When he cabled from London the number of the flight on which he would be arriving, all the customary arrangements had been made. He was met by a KGB embassy guard in an unassuming Renault, his little hotel suite at the Montalembert was booked, and the locked suitcase, stored in the embassy in his absence, was in the room waiting for him. In it he kept a dozen paperback copies of Dostoevski, Tolstoi, Pushkin, Gogol, and several liters of vodka, in plastic containers.

He ordered the cable traffic from European capitals, and from Moscow and Washington, brought in. One, from Moscow, was addressed to him personally. It read: "DID WE PICK UP BLACKFORD OAKES IN PARIS REPLY ILYICH." Bolgin picked up the office telephone and sent for the code clerk. "Bring in Saturday's cables from Washington."

He leafed through them. At 1713 on Saturday, this cable had been received by the Paris chief of station, Sverdlov: "AGENT BLACKFORD OAKES DEPARTED 1000 EDT PANAM FLIGHT #104 DESTINATION PARIS." He did some quick calculation. The transatlantic flight, eastbound, would take ten or eleven hours. Oakes would therefore have arrived in Paris some time after midnight. He picked up the telephone: "Sverdlov." He was put through instantly: "Bolgin. Come, please."

The chief of station, a stocky, light-skinned man wearing an ill-fitting brown suit and gray vest, came to attention in front of Bolgin's desk—Bolgin had the rank of colonel. "Relax." Bolgin waved him toward the chair adjacent, under the picture of Lenin. He passed the cable over to him.

"No, Colonel, we didn't pick him up. We have only that one picture of Oakes, you know. You're the only person in the European theater who has ever seen him, since we lost Erika. The plane was chock-full. We managed to get a look at the manifest, but there was no Oakes listed. So we don't even know what name he's traveling under. And he hasn't been near the U.S. Embassy, which of course isn't surprising."

"Have you begun a hotel search?"

"No, sir. I knew you were coming in, so I thought I'd wait and see whether you wanted to do a search. I am aware, Colonel, of your instructions not to overuse our hotel contacts."

Boris Bolgin tapped his fingers on the desk while he reflected. He pointed to the cable that had just come in. "Moscow wants to know: *Did we pick him up?* What, my dear Sverdlov, do you wish me to reply? *'No.'*—or *'Not yet'?*"

"I understand, sir. You wish the full dragnet?"

"Let me see the picture you have."

Sverdlov reached for the telephone, and presently a stout woman arrived with a folder.

Bolgin looked at it. "Sometimes I cannot understand our Washington office. For three years we have asked for a more up-to-date picture of Oakes. They follow him around even to airports, but they don't bother to get more pictures. It is lucky for them I am not in charge of the Washington office. Still . . . this is only . . . five years old. I don't suppose that handsome fox has grown a beard"—he tugged at his own goatee. He depressed a button and a stenographer came in. "This is to Washington, Seryogin. 'RE OAKES CONTACT ORLY UNMADE. PROCEEDING WITH SEARCH. ADVISE IF HE DEPARTED USING ANY DISGUISE.' " And to Sverdlov: "They won't wake Seryogin up for that, so we won't get an answer until after lunch. Hold up the search until then, so we'll know what we're looking for." Sverdlov rose to go. As he reached the door, Bolgin, while scanning the next cable, said, "By the way, Sverdlov, are you related to the Sverdlov who ordered the execution of the Czar?"

Sverdlov drew his shoulders back. "I have the honor, Colonel, to be his grandson."

"Well, well. Yes. Well, that was a very efficient operation. Yes. Eleven people were there, and we got them all using only seventy-seven bullets."

Sverdlov watched his superior closely, attempting to frame an appropriate reply. He decided to be cautious.

"As you say, Colonel."

That young man will go far, thought Bolgin, waving his finger in dismissal as he returned to the cables.

Chapter 9

SITTING IN the driver's seat of the French taxicab, Blackford Oakes rehearsed yet again what he had gone over so many times with Rufus and Trust. It might very well not work, in which case the alternative plan, concededly less expeditious, would be put into operation the next day. So much depended on whether Soviet-trained Russians *could* act spontaneously. Vadim thought it workable. "On the second hand, I do not know Viksne. If he is one hundred percent the martinet, then we might have our trouble."

"If he's one hundred percent martinet," Rufus had answered, "what would he do? Order another bus? From where? There are no streetcars to the Grand from there. They've *got* to take taxis. It's certainly too far to walk."

Blackford was dressed in a black beret and the blue painter's smock so common among French taxi drivers. He was eating slowly, visibly, from a lunch box and from time to time filling a small glass from an unmarked half liter of red wine. He had resolved that if addressed by anyone he would speak the few words of French he knew in a heavy German accent, there being a couple of dozen Germans who drove cabs in Paris. He thought it unlikely that anyone would accost him, parked as he was by a warehouse on the other side of the street from the Lycée. His Off Duty sign was clearly lit. The seat on his right was hidden by parcels that reached almost to the ceiling of the car. Other parcels occupied a full one third of the rear area. He was apparently engaged in deliveries, taking a quick break for lunch, and not, therefore, available to passengers. He checked, under his dashboard, the battery level of the detonating device and immediately reproached himself for feeling any necessity to do so again, having checked it only fifteen minutes earlier. The route so carefully prepared would take him by a total of fifteen red lights before the access point to the highway. He had rehearsed a driving speed calculated to arrive when each of the lights was green. This required him in some stretches to go as slowly as fifteen miles per hour; in others, as fast as thirty-five miles per hour. In order to activate this schedule, it was required that he pass the first light, at Faubourg St.-Antoine, exactly at midpoint during the full minute it stayed green. On easing into Rue Faidherbe, he could expect to see Trust's blue Mercedes. Blackford would adapt his speed so as to trail the Mercedes, which would stopwatch the preselected maze.

At 12:12 he saw the column of figures walking out of the Lycée toward the bus. The figure in the lead was a man whose picture he had carefully studied—Viksne, a small, chunky man obviously accustomed to giving orders, and to setting the pace. It was warm and sunny but Viksne was amply dressed, vest included, and carried a raincoat in one hand, a briefcase in the other. There followed, in groups of two and three, the dozen scientists and the two interpreters. The scientists carried briefcases, including the girl, Tamara, who walked arm in arm with the lithe, tall, slightly bent-over figure of Viktor Kapitsa. Two of the scientists, wearing cameras about their necks, paused to take pictures, of the Lycée, of themselves, of the bus. They were an animated, but well-harnessed lot. As they walked into the bus, some loitered to permit others to enter first: There is no more rigid hierarchy than in classless societies. Even Viksne was deferring to the venerable Nesmayanov—but no, Viksne was in fact letting all his wards get into the bus before doing so himself, occupying the seat opposite the driver, who cranked up the engine at exactly 12:16. Blackford turned on his motor and eased his Off Duty taxicab behind the bus, keeping a distance of about two thirds of a block.

Down they went, on the Avenue Daumesnil, across the Place Félix Eboué, up the slight rise to the Rue de Reuilly. As the bus approached the Boulevard Diderot, with its hefty, placid apartment buildings on either side, an area where no policemen doing regular duty could be found, Blackford took a breath, put his hand under the dashboard, fingered the toggle switch on the detonating mechanism, and clicked it down. Instantly there was an explosion inside the engine of the bus. It ground to a halt as smoke issued from the motor. The delegation filed out in some excitement; the bus driver gesticulated wildly while attempting to open the hood of the bus without success. Viksne and Nesmayanov were animated as they spoke and one or two cars passed the bus, no one volunteering any help.

Now! thought Blackford—and guided his taxi to that part of the street where Tamara stood, stopping within a foot of her.

Smiling, he said in French: "Where are you headed?"

Tamara looked at Viktor for guidance. Viktor approached the ingratiating languid taxi driver, and in awkward French, managed to say: "To the Hôtel-Grand, at Rue Scribe. Are you by any chance going by there?"

"Sure," said Blackford. "That's on my way. Hop in."

Viktor looked over at Viksne. "Shall I report the breakdown at the hotel?"

"Never mind," Viksne snapped. And, raising his voice to address the other stranded passengers, "Everyone get cabs and we'll meet in the hotel. We'll have a fresh bus for the afternoon session." To Blackford he said in grotesque French, "Can you make room for me?"

"I'm sorry, sir, just two. You can see, I'm delivering parcels."

Tamara stepped in, followed by Viktor, and they began instantly babbling in Russian, although only after Tamara had addressed the driver: *"Merci beaucoup, monsieur."*

Blackford drove forward, recording the time. 12:25:35. It was three minutes, at thirty miles per hour, to that first light on St.-Antoine. It changed on even minutes. He ran his finger down the column of figures on the notebook by his side. He should average either eighteen or thirty-six miles per hour. The fine tuning would be done for him after he arrived at the beginning of the next block —by his escort, Anthony Trust.

And there was the blue Mercedes, moving slowly. To synchronize with it Blackford had to reduce his speed abruptly. He braked, and leaned out the window muttering to a bicyclist something in French which Tamara did not understand, the bicyclist did not understand, and Blackford did not understand; but it motivated the slowdown. The Mercedes picked up speed, as did Blackford.

He had speculated: When would his passengers become suspicious? How would they express their suspicion? Some people come instantly to terms with large cities. Others spend lifetimes visiting them and continue to depend on others to guide them about. Even Vadim did not hazard a guess as to whether Viktor would bother to study the map of Paris. As for Tamara, they had no idea. Certainly, given the distances involved, it would be seven or eight minutes at least before one or the other expressed any concern over the failure to reach the hotel. By that time, five of the fifteen lights would have been passed. Blackford would tell them amiably that one of the packages *had* to be delivered before 12:30, so he was taking a little detour, did they mind? Predictably they would not. If they did, he would go instantly into Phase 3.

It was seven minutes after he had picked them up that Tamara said rather reticently to the driver, "You did understand us to say the Hôtel-Grand? At Scribe and Capucines?"

"Yes, madame. But I must leave"—he pointed to the bulky parcel on top of the heap—"that first at the other address, because they expect it by 12:30. You do not mind a little detour?"

"Certainly not," she said, her lifetime's training in docility taking instant command. And after all, they were in Paris. She resumed her bantering with Viktor.

Five more lights and Blackford popped out of the car, parcel in hand, and smiled. *"Un petit moment!"* Tamara returned the smile. He went around the corner, and deposited the empty parcel in the waste bin.

He returned to the cab and drove off. *Five more lights.* Five more minutes? In fact his passengers did not grow restive until eight full minutes had gone by and clearly they were reaching the outer environs of Paris. This time she was alarmed.

"Where are you taking us?" Her voice was suddenly abrupt.

Blackford reached back with his right hand, and Viktor took from it the proffered envelope. Blackford then electrically elevated a thick glass partition between the front seat and the back seat, and doggedly followed the blue Mercedes, which was now, having passed Porte de Clignancourt, proceeding at over fifty miles per hour on the highway to Chantilly. Upon arriving there, there would be a certain chance of exposure—but not a great deal,

Rufus had reasoned. The window glass in the rear was especially thick. The window handles—and the door handles—did not engage. It would be difficult for the passengers to attract the attention of other motorists. And Anthony's nimble Mercedes, ahead, could provide a certain degree of interference.

Viktor tore open the envelope. The communication was brief and in Russian. It said: "The driver of this car is my friend. Please cooperate with him. Neither you nor Tamara will be hurt." It was signed by a series of numerals. Viktor studied them—and turned excitedly to Tamara.

"Vadim! It is Vadim! Vadim Platov has done this!"

Tamara grabbed her husband by the arm. She extended her hand to the window handle opposite, next to Viktor, and was not surprised that it turned without effect on the window. It was so with the door handle. She sighed. "There isn't anything we can do. We'll have to wait and see."

"I wonder, I wonder," Viktor was talking as if to himself. "Is he trying to arrange it so we can escape? Oh, Vadim, Vadim, you will reintroduce us to the nightmare. I know it." She soothed him though she suspected Viktor was right. And began to suspect that nothing would ever again be the same. Their hearts beat fast when their taxi turned off the highway and went briefly in toward the town of Chantilly. They made no effort to catch the attention of the one or two bystanders they might conceivably have engaged. Viktor began to concentrate on the route the driver had taken. He wondered that he was being permitted to observe the route, the road signs so clearly visible. How easy it would be, when they were released, to find the destination . . . when they were questioned . . . by the police. The French police. Then the KGB. He felt his blood turn to ice, his throat go dry.

"Tamara!" he ordered her. "Close your eyes! Mine are closed. *We don't want to know.* We don't want to know *anything.* One more thing. When we arrive, wherever we are going, say nothing, understand, *nothing!* Let me cope. I don't want anything ever to be attributable to you. *Do you understand!*"

"Yes, my darling."

The car had come to a halt. Blackford opened the passenger door; they stepped into a pebbled driveway in front of a modest chateau surrounded as far as the eye could see by lawns and fields and, down from the front lawn, a small lake with three swans causing the only ripples in that warm, airless July day.

Blackford had removed his beret.

"Won't you come in, Madame Kapitsa, monsieur?"

Blackford turned and walked toward the door. Clutching his briefcase with one hand, his wife with the other, Viktor followed. Inside the hallway Blackford opened the door to a comfortable antechamber, and indicated the way. Tamara accepted her guide's instructions, but when Viktor was about to follow her into the room, Blackford gently detained him.

"Pardon me, monsieur. For just a moment, we must talk with you alone."

Viktor looked at Tamara. She gestured that he should comply. Blackford, engaging Tamara's attention, pointed to the open door of the well-furnished little room, the washroom at the other end, and just then a maid arrived with a tray of tea and sandwiches. Blackford closed the door and led Viktor down the expensively wallpapered hall to a door on the right, which Blackford opened, gesturing to Viktor, who went in, to see standing at the other end of the room, Vadim Platov.

Gently, Blackford closed the door, and walked up the stairs.

Chapter 10

VIKSNE WAS TOO BUSY arranging for a substitute bus to make lunch, arriving at the corner of the huge dining room only as the coffee was being served to his table of scientists. He clicked his fingers at the waitress and instructed her to bring him a plate of "anything"—which she did with manifest distaste, since the hotel prided itself on its cuisine, notwithstanding its great size. The delegates, mostly in pairs, began to drift away to their rooms, preparatory to reassembling for the longish bus trip to the Lycée at Vincennes in fifteen minutes. Nesmayanov tarried, and now he was alone with his coffee and Viksne, who was stuffing bread and rolls and cheese into his mouth and gulping down red wine.

"Is Kapitsa with you?" the academician asked.

"With me?" Viksne said, his mouth full of food. "I have been steadily on the telephone—to the arrangements bureau of the embassy, and directly to the bus company, for"—he looked at his watch—"forty-five minutes!"

"In that case he is missing."

Viksne stopped eating. "He did not come to lunch?"

"That is correct, nor Tamara."

"Was there any comment?"

"Yes. They normally sit down at the end of the table next to

Dyakov. Dyakov said something about how we'd all better take the opportunity to tell our inventory of dirty jokes, since Tamara was not here. Someone asked where they were, and Dyakov said he assumed they were assisting you."

Viksne rose, his plate half full. "We'll leave it at that. *That's the story*. They were helping me. I asked them to help superintend the bus replacement, Tamara's knowledge of French makes her especially useful. I am going now to phone the embassy. If I am not in the lobby at 1430, escort the delegation to the Lycée and I'll meet you there by taxi. Remember: *silence*." Nesmayanov had reached the age when he knew how to deal with KGB officials: acquiescently. He nodded.

Viksne went to his own room to telephone. Sverdlov, he learned, was out to lunch. Did he wish to speak to Colonel Bolgin? the operator asked. He considered briefly. To do so might be to give unnecessary alarm. To fail to act while Sverdlov was lunching, on the other hand, might later be condemned as lackadaisical. Better to go right to Bolgin. "Yes."

Bolgin came on the line, listened.

"Have you ordered an investigation of the bus?"

"No, sir. I had no reason to suspect . . ."

"Call back this office and advise where the bus is located at this moment. One of our technicians will go down to inspect it. Get the hotel to let you into Kapitsa's room—tell them he asked you to bring some papers he left behind. Examine the room thoroughly and tell me if there are any leads. Either he has defected, or he has been abducted."

"I do not think he would defect, Colonel. He is the essence of docility; so is Tamara. Moreover, he is tremendously excited by the advances on our . . . project. He was even reluctant to come because it would take him from his work for one week, even though he knows there is nothing he can do in the immediate period to accelerate our . . . project."

"Just how indispensable is he to the project?"

"On one aspect of it, Colonel, he has been the key figure. But that work is done. We cannot know who will crack the remaining barrier."

"I shall decide whether to report this to the French authorities. Meanwhile *no one* is to know. Tell the delegation his wife has taken ill and he is at her side. Is he scheduled to read today?"

"No, sir. His lecture is tomorrow afternoon."

"We'll have a course of action well before then. I shall advise Moscow immediately. I'll expect a call from you within fifteen minutes." Bolgin hung up.

At 3:15 a telephone call to Bolgin from the garage confirmed that the bus had been stopped by a low-powered explosive. At 3:20, while Bolgin was in the coding room preparing his message for Moscow, there was a knock at the door, a distraction no one had ever before been guilty of. Flushed, he rose, and unlocked the massive door.

It was the ambassador, who beckoned to Bolgin, worldlessly, to follow him. They walked up one flight of stairs to the special chamber in the embassies of the superpowers where conversation takes place inside an electromagnetically insulated room which is proof against all known interceptive technology. Ambassador Yevgeny Silin, an old-timer, had been en route to Moscow the very day Stalin died—because it had been Stalin's twitchy moribund velleity to liquidate Silin. But after Stalin's death no member of his staff could come up with what it was that Silin might have done, or failed to have done, to antagonize the great leader; so Silin, having been examined by Beria, Bolgin, and Molotov, all of them his contemporaries, was sent back to Paris, where he continued to serve, enhancing, year after year, his reputation for personal wit and a dumb servility to his superiors.

"Have a look, Boris. It was delivered to my desk five minutes ago."

Bolgin looked first at the envelope. It was of first-quality paper, without return address. And, typed on its face: "FOR THE IMMEDIATE PERSONAL ATTENTION OF HIS EXCELLENCY THE AMBASSADOR. ANY DELAY IN DELIVERING THIS COULD PROVE FATAL."

"A little boy gave it to the guard. Someone in a taxi gave it to the boy with a hundred francs. Doesn't know who, couldn't identify him, etc., etc."

Bolgin took the sheet of paper from the envelope and read.

> Your Excellency:
> We address you on behalf of the embattled people of Algeria who are fighting a war of independence under trying conditions. Your country is the leading socialist nation in the world, the self-proclaimed friend of all who struggle in the wars of national liberation. We have heard the encouraging words of Soviet leaders. But what

else? Your representatives, in Cairo, in Tunis, indeed in Paris, have repeatedly promised a substantial shipment of arms. And now we learn that the *Chekhov,* scheduled to sail from Sebastopol at midnight tonight, is not in fact bringing military relief to our fellow Algerians, but has been instructed to proceed to Indonesia. Why does Sukarno have priority?

We cannot wait any longer. We are men and women of action. We have in our custody one of your top scientists. Unless you reroute the *Chekhov* and make the arms delivery to Algeria, he will not be returned to you. What our disposition of him will then be presents many interesting possibilities, which will no doubt occur to you as well as to us.

You may summon the police, as you like. You may advise the world press, as you like. The press cannot hurt us, the police cannot find us. Should it happen that anyone did find us, we are pledged to die, together with M. Kapitsa and his wife.

We shall watch the personal columns of *Le Monde.* We shall look for a message that begins: "My beloved Anna Krupskaya." All we desire to read is: "I promise to respect your wishes by . . ." You may here supply the exact date and approximate hour when the *Chekhov* can be expected to arrive at Bizerte, where the captain will be contacted by a reliable person. Immediately upon the off-loading of the shipment, you will see again the Kapitsas. We estimate that the entire operation need not take more than four days.

We wish you to know, moreover, that when the revolutionary government of Algeria is established, we shall see to it that the cost of your arms is reimbursed.

The letter closed: "For the FLN" and, signed in red ink, simply, "Jean."

Bolgin asked: "Any idea who it is?"

"I was going to ask you, my dear Boris. This is certainly your . . . beat."

"The KGB does not object to our diplomats learning the identity of enterprising Algerian terrorists, Mr. Ambassador"—the form of address was a rebuke: but mild. Silin knew that Bolgin also knew that the upheavals within the FLN since the kidnapping of Ben Bella a year before had made communication with effective authority within the Algerian movement difficult; more accurately, impossible.

"For a socialist revolution, Colonel"—he reciprocated the formality—"the FLN is the closest thing to an anarchist operation since the Narodniki. Nobody appears to know whom to deal with. The French do not know to whom to tender offers of negotiation. Individual Algerian leaders command strikes, acts of terrorism, abductions. It is altogether chaotic. There is no easy way of knowing who Jean is or whether he acted on his own authority."

"Whoever he is, I wouldn't mind hiring him when this is all over. I envy his familiarity with shipping schedules in Sebastopol." Bolgin paused, detachedly wondering just *how that* information had got out—he was not himself aware of it. He made a note to probe Moscow. "In the event you were not aware of it, Mr. Ambassador, Kapitsa is critical to an ongoing scientific operation to which the Kremlin attaches the highest priority."

"May I ask why, under the circumstances, you let him out of the country?"

Bolgin thumped his hand down on the table. "Please! Do not affect to pretend that it is KGB-Europe that decides these matters. He came pursuant to Politburo designs, with a KGB-Moscow escort who concededly did not provide adequate protection. To be sure, the abduction was carried out with extraordinary skill. I have Viksne, the escort official, seeing what he can do to track down the taxi. But apparently that will prove unlikely. The whole thing was done quickly, in hectic circumstances brilliantly contrived. The question is how to reply to 'Jean.'"

"What we say is obviously for Moscow to decide."

"Of course. Moscow decides everything, from world war to whether you are paying too much for your mistress." Silin blanched. Bolgin enjoyed occasional manifestations of his omniscience. "And that goes also for the question of whether to bring in the French police. I have my own opinion on the matter, but let me have yours: What are the chances of getting Sûreté Nationale without the press catching on?"

"I should think about fifty-fifty. The French sometimes effect discreet operations with considerable skill. They managed, you will remember, not very long ago to mount a fair-sized war in the

Suez without the knowledge of either President Eisenhower or Comrade Khrushchev."

Bolgin tensed at this reminder of the major delinquency of his career. Silin did not rub it in. He went on: "On the other hand, the censorship of Algerian events is very disorderly, and informers are well paid by the press. I can accordingly not make a judgment one way or the other. The arguments would, in my view, weigh heavily in favor of bringing in the French. They have their own informants in Algerian circles. Either we make an effort to liberate Kapitsa, which means bringing in the French, or we lie down and give them the arms."

"Thank God for Moscow."

"Thank who, Colonel?"

Bolgin rose. "I shall code Moscow directly."

"Are you, Colonel Bolgin, formally relieving me of personal responsibility in this situation?"

"I am. Subject to Moscow's specifying your duties." The ambassador rose, tripped the lock, and led the way out of the chamber.

* * *

Bolgin, alone in the code room minutes later, thought feverishly for a moment. He picked up the telephone and reached Sverdlov. "Establish immediately the deadline for personals in tomorrow's edition of *Le Monde*." He put down the telephone and wondered—wondered what everyone wondered who initiated a distress call to Moscow: Would they blame him? Security arrangements for foreign trips are strictly the business of KGB-Moscow. But the advantage of being KGB-Moscow is that you can shift the blame to others. What hellish luck that he happened to be in Paris at the moment. Though they'd almost certainly have called him in from London in any case.

He went to work, using his personal code, and relaying the story in full.

Chapter 11

JÓZSEF NADY had specified that Frieda and Erno should meet that night not at their regular meeting place, the restaurant L'Ancien Franz, but at his little apartment on Avenue Ingres. They convened frequently with other refugees of the Hungarian uprising at bars and restaurants, meetings at times lugubrious, at times buoyant, according as the mood, dictated by random rumor, was good or bad. The three were especially close, bound by personal ties to Theophilus Molnar, with whom they had matriculated at the university and conspired in the months and days before that glorious short-lived week in October. When the tanks came on the Sunday morning before dawn, they had been asleep. They made their way out of Budapest on Thursday, through the contact at the candy shop on Ferenc Street, the owner of which had passed on to them the day before the harrowing details of the execution of Theophilus. It was József who reasoned that manifestly Theo had been betrayed by the American, known to them as "Harry." József told them he had defied the curfew the night of the execution. He told Frieda and Erno that if Harry had still been at the hotel, "there would be one less traitor alive in Budapest." But Blackford Oakes had checked out. József managed to intimidate the concierge into letting him look at the registration book.

József copied it down: "Harry E. Browne, 34 St. Ronan Street, New Haven, Connecticut. Passport number H 2452463, issued in New York on July 6, 1956." The following night they assembled at Madame Zlaty's store near the university, where a contact from the resistance, driving a milk wagon, would pick them up at dawn the next morning. They emerged from the shop dressed as dairy workers. That night they spent on a farm twenty kilometers from the city. The next night they were in Vienna. Two weeks later they arrived in Paris, having deliberated—and rejected as too far distant from home—the United States as an alternative sanctuary. József betrayed an antipathy to the United States which he associated with the despised "Harry." Frieda, listless since hearing of the fate of Theo, had smiled appreciatively, and put her arm around the shoulders of József, whose loyalty to her dead fiancé was so ardent.

Frieda and Erno arrived simultaneously. She was beginning to climb the stairs, tired after a long day at the typewriter of the firm of Coudert Frères. Erno, who worked the graveyard shift as a linotypist for *Le Monde* and was relatively fresh, greeted her affectionately.

"Wonder what's up?" he said as they climbed the stairs to 4A. She depressed the button using the old rhythmic dash dot dot dash they had used during the exhilarating months almost exactly a year ago. Instantly József opened the door, hugged Frieda, and offered his hand to Erno. He waved them into his small sitting room with the wilted couch and chair, disappeared into the kitchen, brought out a bottle of chilled white wine, poured, sat down, and said:

"Harry is in Paris and I know where he is!"

Both his listeners put down their glasses. "Tell us," said Frieda quietly, her large brown eyes closing with concentration.

"I was delivering a radio we had repaired at the shop to the housekeeper of the Hôtel France et Choiseul. As I walked into the service entrance, *he* walked out of the guest entrance, and into a car, a gray Citroën. I have the license number."

"Are you sure it was Harry?" Erno asked.

"Is there anybody else who looks like Harry?"

"That's true," Frieda reflected. "Nobody else looks like Harry. . . . What shall we do?"

"We could turn him in to the French police," Erno suggested.

"And what would *they* do?" József snorted. "In the first place we can't prove he's a Soviet agent. In the second place if we did, all they would do is kick him out of the country. After all, he's an American citizen."

"We could tell the Americans about him."

"Ah yes," József said, "I agree. I think we should do that—after."

"After what?" Frieda asked.

"After we avenge Theo."

Erno's voice turned cold. "What do you propose, József?"

"I propose that we hang him by the neck until he is as dead as Theophilus. Then we will see to it that the United States—and the Communists—know that although Hungary is enslaved, not all Hungarians are slaves."

Frieda thought back on her quiet and gentle Theo, a tiger on the soccer field and, sometimes, in her bed: but otherwise calm, purposeful, joyfully convinced of a future free of domination, of political trials, of torture, execution, exile. A great bitterness welled up in her, as she recalled József's account, taken from the concierge, of Theo's execution.

"I agree," she said, uttering the words slowly, emphatically. "But on this condition: We must let him speak. Not like Theo. And—if he prays—give him time to pray unlike Theo."

József turned to Erno.

"I too agree. But how? Shooting him when he approaches the hotel is something we might arrange. But *hanging* him . . ."

"I have thought of little else since I saw him," József said. "I tipped the doorman and told him I suspected the American was playing around with my girl, and I wanted to check her excuses, and would he keep his eyes on Harry. He promised he would. Then I called reception and said that the cuff links ordered by Mr. Harry Browne's mother from New Haven as a surprise gift for her son's birthday would not be ready for ten days; was that too late? He checked and told me Mr. Browne had reservations for the whole month of July."

"That doesn't answer the question of how we will get hold of him."

"I have that figured out. I'll go to the garage with a work order from the store to repair the radio in the gray Citroën Plate 467-H. The garage superintendent has his office in the entrance. The exit is at the other end of the building. After a half hour I will leave with my tool chest and wave good-bye to the superintendent.

I shall reenter the garage from the exit side and go right to the car and lie on the floor of the back seat."

"What if Harry sees you when he gets into the car?"

"He won't. If by any chance he did, I'd pretend I was sleeping off a drunk and wobble out with my tool kit. You will be parked in a rented car at the corner of Castiglione and St.-Honoré and when you see the gray Citroën with that license plate, you will follow us. I'll move on him within two minutes of the time he turns out of the garage and put this"—he lifted a .38 revolver from under the cushion of the couch—"behind the back of his neck and tell him if he wants to stay alive to follow my instructions exactly."

"Where do we take him?"

"Do you remember the picnic on Independence Day when we drove to Fontainebleau?"

"Of course," said Frieda. "Off the road and deserted. Perfect."

Erno wondered whether they should bring along any more of their compatriots, but agreed finally with József that there was always a risk. "Besides, we three had a special relationship with Theo."

And so it was left that József, having been tipped off by the doorman, would estimate the likeliest time of departure of Harry Browne from the hotel, and the plan would go instantly into action.

"You, Erno," said József, "need to bring the rope. We will tie his hands behind him when we take him out of the car." Frieda gave an involuntary shudder but bit her lips, and although she had tried for six months to drive out of her mind the picture of Theo swinging in the wind on the gibbet of the rattling truck, now she ushered the image back into her mind, and instantly recovered her resolution. József, sweating with excitement, pursed his lips and shook his head with its light blond hair ferociously. "Perhaps now they will learn something!"

Erno walked over to the bookcase, on top of which was a framed picture. It was taken of Theophilus holding the soccer cup in his freshman year. "To my great friend József, Theo."

"I'm with you all the way," Erno said.

"And I," echoed Frieda.

Chapter 12

WELL, BOLGIN THOUGHT as he put down the receiver: At least *something* isn't going sour! He looked at his watch. He didn't like to make appointments for 8 P.M. That put off his dinner-vodka hour. But under the pressure of the Kapitsa matter he would in any event need to be alert until about ten, even though Moscow had ended a furious series of chaotic messages by saying that no communication would be ready for *Le Monde*'s six o'clock deadline that day, Tuesday, for Wednesday's editions. The Algerian kidnappers would have to wait at least until Thursday. Meanwhile Viksne was instructed to advise the scientific delegation that the Kapitsas had been taken into the Soviet ambassador's residence, where Tamara was being treated for what appeared to be an acute dysentery from which her husband was also suffering slightly. His scheduled lecture at the Lycée the following day would be read, on his behalf, by one of his colleagues. The French police were NOT REPEAT NOT to be advised of the disappearance of Kapitsa. (Bolgin, after Stalin died, indulged himself in a parody on one occasion when he cabled Ilyich: "THE APPROACH TO MENDÈS-FRANCE HAS NOT REPEAT NOT UNREPEAT PREVIOUS REPEAT NOT BEEN SUCCESSFUL." The reply from Ilyich, who had been his classmate at the NKVD Academy a generation earlier, could roughly be paraphrased as: "STALIN IS NOT DEAD." It had been transmitted in the person-to-person code, and had said, in earthy Russian, quite simply: "BORIS, CUT THE SHIT." Boris Bolgin never needed to be told anything twice.)

The bus company was to be compensated fully, rendering any intrusion by insurance agents unnecessary. In short, no one not already aware of the disappearance of the Kapitsas should be made privy to it. The text to be given to *Le Monde* would be cabled the following morning after further deliberation in the Kremlin. Bolgin was advised that the *Chekhov* would depart Sebastopol on schedule. Whether it would turn east toward the Suez Canal and Indonesia after leaving the Aegean—or west toward Tunis—would be decided tomorrow, with appropriate instructions radioed to the captain. Meanwhile, the duty officer at the embassy should be apprised of Bolgin's whereabouts around the clock.

* * *

Fair enough, thought Bolgin, reaching for his fedora. By ten o'clock Paris time it would be midnight in Moscow. Now that You-Know-Who, with his lunatic passion for meetings at two, three in the morning, isn't running the country, the chances that anybody would want to be in touch with him after Moscow-midnight were too remote to worry about. Along about midnight, the alcohol would be lifting Boris from Dostoevski, like a secondary launch, rising—slowly, at first, then with a giddily accelerating velocity—into the stratosphere; and Boris would know blankness, peace, until he woke.

Meanwhile he had some heavy gloating to do. He looked at his watch in the dimly lit restaurant. He ordered black coffee and mineral water and took up the afternoon paper. But his mind wandered. Sverdlov—you had to give him credit—had done a good job. At three the dragnet had gone out. One of the agents, sitting in the lobby of the France et Choiseul, spotted Blackford Oakes leaving the hotel lobby that very afternoon. The agent followed him out and saw him get into the Citroën, whose license number he memorized. He was registered in the hotel under the name of Harry Browne. "Ah, Blackford," Bolgin thought. "This time, my friend, I have got you, oh yes I do, my friend Blackford, oh yes I do!" He was very nearly smiling when the young man unobtrusively sat down beside him. To the waiter the young man said, "Do you have any Hungarian beer?"

The waiter nodded, "Dreher."

"*Bien.*" He turned to Bolgin, who addressed him in English.

"Do I suppose it goes well with your friends?"

"It went exactly as we planned."

"Very well. Now, let us reflect for a little moment. We know that Oakes was very indispensable to finance and to organize the contact points for Hungarian escapees. In six months we have exterminated three of them—yours, of course, we finished as soon as we got your message in Vienna. But we couldn't get anything out of the old lady about the others. She did not know, or she would not talk: We'll not know ever which at this point. Ah, a tough business, eh József?

"Now, our friend Oakes, he will of course insist to your colleagues that he is innocent. Are you quite certain your . . . friends . . . they are convinced it was Oakes who gave us the address on Dohany Street?"

"Quite certain—though they know him only as 'Harry.' I led them to that conclusion the very night of the execution. I told them that Theo had told me his American friend had given him a special address on Dohany, but that Theo never gave me the number on that street. They are absolutely convinced it was Harry."

"Good! To prove himself innocent it isn't certain what he will attempt. But we know what we desire. Yes, of course, we desire anything you can get from him that would pleasingly surprise us. For instance, any special contacts in Paris. Information on any operations he might be doing. What would help is if he told you where the other contacts are in Budapest that are still operating. Because the girl Frieda and your other friend, I forget his name . . . ?"

"Erno. Erno Toth."

". . . they might, Oakes will calculate, know that he is telling the truth if he gives the names and locations of the contacts—they might have heard about one or two or three of those contact points from other refugees."

"I doubt it. The refugees are all tight-lipped. You know that. I haven't had any successes for you on that front."

"Well," Bolgin said, sipping his glass of water, "a man gets pretty desperate when he is walking toward the hanging rope, eh József? I am certain Mr. Oakes will think of *something* worth you repeating to me."

József smiled. "What shall we do when he is talked out, Colonel?"

"What shall you do? Why, my dear József, you will hang Mr. Oakes. Yes"—Bolgin raised his glass of mineral water as if to toast the idea—"Moscow would like that. In fact"—his eyebrows came together—"Bolgin would like that! You will of course take a photograph. You will say to your confederates it is essential for the morale of the 'Freedom Fighters,' eh? But also—and you will *not* say," he chuckled, "essential for the morale of Moscow, and excellent for the morale of Bolgin. The morale of Bolgin is also worth some maintaining, is it not true, József?" Bolgin laughed almost convulsively. "Blackford Oakes, the picture-poster secret star of the great Central Intelligence Agency. Hanged as a traitor—by the Hungarian Freedom Fighters Oakes helped escape from Hungary! It is too delicious. We shall see that it gets leaked, gets worldwide leaked! Do you ever see the *National Review,* József?"

József said that although he read several American periodicals, he did not read *National Review.*

"It is edited by this young bourgeois fanatic. Oh, how they cried about the repression of the counterrevolutionaries in Budapest! But the *National Review,* it is angry also with the CIA for —I don't know, not starting up a Third World War, maybe? Last week—I always read the *National Review,* it makes me so funny-mad—last week an editorial said"—he raised his head and appeared to quote from memory—"'The attempted assassination of Sukarno last week had all the earmarks of a CIA operation. Everybody in the room was killed except Sukarno.'" Bolgin roared, and suddenly wished his mineral water were vodka. Should he order some? *No!* No, a thousand times no! He marshaled his thought. His features returned to pop-Bolshevik: "We will distribute that picture," he said soberly. "'Hungarian Freedom Fighters/Execute U.S. CIA Agent/Caught Collaborating with KGB.' Such black eyes for our friends in the CIA, no, József?"

"Yes! Terrific! . . . Say, Colonel. You know, it is getting very expensive, life in Paris. And I do need my own automobile. Renting one from time to time for specific missions, well, it isn't entirely satisfactory."

Bolgin, prepared, reached into his pocket and extended his hand under the table.

"What you find in this envelope there will be five times of when the photograph comes to me."

Chapter 13

"I AM VERY SORRY, Dean. Did Martha bring you tea? Ah yes; I see she did." The Director of the Central Intelligence Agency poured himself a cup and sat down. "In the situation I was in it would have been awkward to tell anybody 'Please call Dean Acheson and tell him I'll be late.'"

"*Pace.* I know how those things are," the tall distinguished figure with the waxed moustache replied in drawling Grotonian. "I have been enjoying the afternoon paper. It recounts the inside story of the shake-up in the Kremlin. Molotov led the fight against Khrushchev, charging that he had been a failure in foreign policy. Poor old Molotov," the former Secretary sighed exaggeratedly. "Obviously the Ribbentrop-Molotov Pact went to his head. As a perfectionist, he cannot stand lesser diplomacy." His eyes were still on the paper. "Hmm . . . Molotov out. Malenkov out. Kaganovich out. At this rate, Allen, I shall soon be left without any personal friends in the Presidium."

The Director laughed, stirred his tea, and said then, gravely, "It was a very long meeting, Dean, and tension is building."

"Do you wish to tell me about it?" That obviously was exactly what the Director wished to do, else why would he have asked especially to see him after the National Security Council meeting?

The Director stirred his tea for a minute, and got up to turn off the air conditioning. "You may remember my telling you after the May Day exhibition that our analysts were tempted to conclude that the next big phase in Soviet strategic armament would center on long-range bombers. They flew nine of those huge Bisons over Moscow in tight formation—that's a hell of an airplane, the equivalent of our B-52. Some of our people projected they'd bypass rockets, for one armament generation in any case, and go heavy with the airplanes. So we sent out orders to our spotters: 'Bring in as much information as you can to point us in the right direction.' We want to know, for instance, how many Bisons have they actually got."

"Do you have the answer?"

"As far as we can figure out, they have nine. In other words, they flew their entire goddam fleet over Moscow."

"Don't swear, Allen."

"Is that what you used to tell Harry Truman?"

"Presidents are allowed to swear. Second Samuel 19, Verse 23."

"Now of course we don't *know* this for sure, but there certainly aren't a lot of Bisons, and they don't seem to be coming off the assembly lines."

"Do I take it our President is reconciled to a little skywatching? And has your brother the Secretary of State found any theological objections?"

The Director laughed. "You'd think Ike had invented the U-2 himself. You remember he only grudgingly allowed us to *produce* it, said he doubted he'd ever permit us to *use* it. He's got now so he's absolutely hooked on the U-2 reports."

"You mean he prefers them to Zane Grey?"

"Oh come off it, Dean. Ike didn't become General of the Army by specializing in military ignorance."

"That's true. He specialized in other forms of ignorance."

"Shall I go on?" The Director was mildly exasperated.

"Sorry."

"Anyway, as you know, we've been tracking Kapistan Yar for a couple of years. Total radar monitoring of all their rocket activity, which has been progressing, but without any spectacular breakthrough. Well, last week our birdie, coming in from Peshawar in Pakistan to Adana in Turkey, photographed some interesting stuff, which we have developed, and which was the reason for the special meeting this afternoon. Remember the name 'Tyura Tam.' By contrast, Kapistan Yar is a Potemkin Village."

"Where is Tyura Tam?"

"It's 680 miles east of Kapistan Yar, on the Trans-Siberian Railroad. They need the railroad because of the weight of the fuel and rockets. The base is sixty miles by ten miles, on a line extending from the northern tip of the Aral Sea"—the Director pulled out an atlas, ran his eye over the table of contents, opened it, and put it in front of his friend—"to the middle of Lake Balkhash. The big stuff is there: sixty- to seventy-foot-tall missiles. They look bloody well ready to go."

"How does a missile look 'ready to go'?"

"The assumptions are based on comparative appearance. If you get a dozen missiles in a row, a mile between missiles, comparisons will tell you those on which work has been apparently completed. These missiles use the RD-107 as the basic launch vehicle. There is no doubt in our minds that at least one or maybe more of those missiles is designed to launch an earth satellite. That satellite is intended to electrify the world—which it will, if it's the first one—and the achievement of that one launch will establish beyond any doubt that the bombers were a ruse—that the highest priority and the best brains in Russia have been devoted to developing an international ballistics missile powerful enough to lift their heavy thermonuclear heads but also smart enough to guide them to any target within a projected range of 5,500 miles."

"Does that mean Texas would still be safe?"

"Well, yes."

"Too bad."

"The effect of that satellite—a symbol of a burgeoning technology that threatens Soviet strategic preeminence—can't be exaggerated. However, they are stumped on one thing."

"What is it? Don't tell me if you don't want to."

"They are stumped because they don't know how to increase the power of—I'm using layman's language—"

"Why not? After all you *are* a layman."

". . . increase the power of the transistor crystals. Without that power the satellite, even if launched, would be uncontrollable, would emit no durable radio signal, and would be useless in accumulating and recording scientific data."

"Is this crystal business you speak of something we know how to do?"

"It is, thank God. And we came on it quite by accident. Courtesy of the private enterprise system, as it happens. Moreover, Dean, as we sit here, the Soviet Union—if only it knew—could pick up something called a Van de Graaff. Van de Graaff, by the way, isn't a seventeenth-century Dutchman. He's a live MIT professor. The machine is manufactured, of all places, in Massachusetts. The unit is about the size of a Volkswagen, costs a couple of hundred thousand dollars, and increases the potency of transistors by means of an electron beam bombardment that irregularizes transistor crystals."

"I don't understand that."

"Neither do I. I'm just telling you: That's *all* they're missing. They simply don't know that the irregularization of transistor crystals can increase their potency by a factor of one hundred. A fifty-cent transistor can be turned into a thirty-dollar transistor by passing through a Van de Graaff."

"How do you know they don't have it?"

"That's something, Dean, I *do* mind telling you."

"Very well. How long would your people guess before they crack it?"

"That's the damnedest thing. We *don't know*. Conceivably they could come on the thing tomorrow. But then conceivably they could poke about six, eight, ten months before getting it. And by *that* time we should get our birdie up there."

"What's holding us up?"

"Agreement on the right blend of launching fuel. There are advocates of just about every combination. We were able to guess when we took a hard look at the size of the Russian rockets, and checked the performance of their western base, that they've licked the fuel problem. We only just now have an inkling of what it is they are on to."

"Yes?"

"Liquefied ozone. Liquid ozone is something the rocket-types sometimes call 'supercharged oxygen.' Ozone that hasn't been liquefied is incredibly dangerous and erratic. Our Dr. Dornberger has said he wouldn't stand several miles from any launch site using liquid oxygen and liquid hydrogen. Ozone, in a liquid form, they have thought of as ideal—if it could be distilled in totally pure form. Ideal in terms of withstanding vibration, heat, impact. One guy not long ago thought he had perfected a 100 percent pure liquid ozone—which promptly exploded. (He died, by the way,

Dean, intestate.) It looks as though the Russians have developed a means of stabilizing ozone for liquid-fueled monster rockets. And it looks as though we will eventually learn how to do this. Once we've got it, using just the ozone, or a combination, we can go."

"So what it comes down to is: They need the Van de Graaff. We need, so to speak, their ozone formula."

"That's a fair way to put it."

"And we think we're about to discover the ozone formula, but they know nothing about Van de Graaff?"

"That's an optimistic way of putting it."

"Well, you put it your way."

"I am telling you something known to the President and six— now seven—Americans. Which is that we hope by the end of this week to have the ozone formula."

"Once we get it, how long before we can fire?"

"We figure, as closely as possible, six to eight months."

"How long would it take them to go if they got the Van de Graaff?"

"Two weeks."

The former Secretary paused. "It is obvious what we want and what we don't have."

"Correct. One cannot exaggerate the importance of going up first with a satellite. It will affect our diplomacy, the way we are regarded, in every chancellery in the world. Are you agreed?"

"I am agreed. It would take a long time to overcome a technological setback of that kind. It might, incidentally, very easily decide the next presidential election."

"You mean, the 'stupid' party could be voted out?"

"I didn't say that, Allen." He smiled. "Besides, Democrats often wage stupid campaigns. What can I do for you, my friend?"

"I speak now on behalf of my brother and the President. Will you, early in the fall, take a trip? London, Paris, Bonn, Rome. The purpose: to advise our friends that the Soviet Union is going to go big for rocketry. That the United States is doing solid work on rocketry and confidently expects to launch a satellite ahead of the Soviet Union. That a Soviet satellite will not, however, be delayed for very long, but that our massive technological resources will in any case cause us to forge ahead and extend that lead over the next two or three years, and that as a leading Democrat you are quite confident that the Democrats in Congress will vote the necessary funds."

His guest pulled a leather book out of his pocket and leafed through a few pages.

"I will be in Europe in November. Is that soon enough?"

"That may be stretching it. Could you possibly move it forward? October?"

He studied the book. "Hmm. Judge Lorenzo, before whom I am scheduled to litigate in October, is, I believe, a Republican appointee. He has—up until now?"—one tip of the famous moustache cocked up quizzically—"adamantly declined any further postponements."

The Director took out his pencil.

"What court?"

"District Court, D.C."

"Consider it done."

The visitor stood up, shook hands, and walked toward the door. "It's bad news they are making such progress. But you appear to have done a good job of intelligence. Well done."

"Thank you."

"Someday your spy network may discover poverty in America, and do something about it."

"There can't be that many poor people, Dean. They all voted for your party—and look how many votes you got."

The former Secretary smiled, and they shook hands.

Chapter 14

THE IDEA WAS to leave them alone. There were contingency arrangements. "The Worst Case situation," Rufus had lectured Blackford, Anthony Trust, and Vadim, "is if Kapitsa raises unshirted hell, refuses to speak to his old friend, clams up, demands the police, the ambassador, the whole works. If that happens, then we cover our losses. Vadim will apologize, tell him he, Vadim, felt he had to make an effort to give Viktor and Tamara a choice, that to that end he got a couple of friends with anti-Communist backgrounds to help him out, that he hadn't tipped off any U.S.A. officials because no one from America would cooperate in any such enterprise especially on foreign soil; that Vadim will arrange to get him back to Paris, and he can tell the Russians he persuaded the Algerian kidnappers they would be much better off letting him argue the case for aid to Algeria in person than as a prisoner. End—we hope—of an unsuccessful episode.

"Going to the *other* extreme, there's the possibility that Kapitsa will welcome the opportunity to defect—don't interrupt me, Vadim—we're talking *hypothetical* possibilities. In *that* event we are ready to move with great speed to get him out of the country. At this end we can tie up the Russians by stretching out the Algerians' demands for a few days and then telling them that Dr.

Kapitsa has escaped. They will guess either that he defected or that he was killed. Let them guess."

Rufus stood up, and there began one of his renowned pauses, during which his three auditors maintained a disciplined silence. Finally he resumed.

"A third possibility strikes me as the likeliest, on the basis of what Vadim has told us about Kapitsa. It is that on the one hand he won't turn against his old friend here resentfully—particularly when Vadim tells him that he arranged the elaborate cover story assigning responsibility to the Algerians. But that he will want to go back to Russia. We just don't know. But Vadim is in a position to tell him, gently but with some firmness, that Kapitsa *must* agree to stay in the chateau and think it over for at least forty-eight hours, that for one thing the cover story would stand up better if there was a delay of at least that long. During those forty-eight hours, Vadim must labor as best he can to get the most information out of him. Will he tell us what they are up to in Tyura Tam? When do they expect to go with the satellite? What's holding them up? What can he tell us about the fuel mix they're going to use? Have they had any success in purifying ozone? *Everything* we can get out of him. There is, further, the remote possibility that he would be willing to return to Russia—and feed us information on a regular basis. This, for us, is obviously the ideal result, better than a defection. To make that arrangement raises the question of Tamara. And my guess is, Vadim, that you shouldn't even raise it as a possibility until you and Viktor are entirely alone. You should try to be alone with him as long as you can when you first meet. Then bring in the girl, have dinner, make them feel at home. You'll be excellently fed. They will see only the French maid, and the cook, if they wander into the kitchen. Trust will be in the east wing and will stay there to take any communications from Vadim. Blackford, you will supervise the delivery of the ransom message to the Soviet Embassy, come back to me, and report on the success of the initial proceedings. Then return to the hotel until I tell you to go back out to Chantilly. You will check with me, using a pay phone, the next morning and we'll discuss what we find in *Le Monde*. I'll give you any information I've gotten from Trust."

* * *

And Blackford had done just that, and then repaired to a public telephone booth. Rufus was pleased that the operation had in its first phase gone smoothly. He informed Blackford that Trust had already called in from Chantilly to say that his "guest" was acting very "reasonably"—which meant he was not resisting his sequestration. "By the way, Blackford," Rufus went on, "your old friend Bolgin is in town. Left London two days ago, we've learned. So he'll be managing the case here on the spot. There's nothing to do now until tomorrow morning. You may as well go out and taste the smells and sights of Paris."

"Rufus!"

Rufus ignored this, saying merely, "Call me in the morning. Let us say . . . between nine-thirty and ten. I'll have a report from Trust." He hung up.

Trust! Ah, Anthony. Blackford remembered his own report. . . . Last night, at the chateau, after Vadim had gone to bed, they had chatted. Toward the end of the evening Anthony had said, "Do you remember Doucette?"

"My dear Anthony, I dimly remember Doucette. I am quite certain that she remembers me."

"Well, Doucette has a younger sister. I . . . 'met' her sister over the weekend."

"At Madame Pensaud's?"

"Madame Pensaud has gone to her reward."

"Ouch!"

"But as you know in France tradition is everything. Madame Pensaud's niece is the current entrepreneur, and her quarters and facilities are unchanged, including the picture of Queen Caroline, and the diatribe against the Fourth Republic. But Doucette's sister, she confided to me—"

"Is that all she did to you?"

"Quiet, Oakes: I am about to share a treasure with you."

"Anthony, before you share any treasures with me, may I ask when you last had a checkup?"

"This's hardly the way to treat your old benefactor, Blackford. Anyway, Doucette's sister, Alouette, slipped me her telephone number, telling me that it was 'more convenient' all the way around that way."

"In other words, she doesn't have to share the boodle with Madame."

"Oakes, you should be in Intelligence."

"I would prefer to be in Alouette."

"Moreover, you have not lost your distinctive vulgarity."

"I'll discuss my distinctions with Alouette."

They had been interrupted—the maid came in to ask if there would be anything else before she retired—but Blackford had in fact absentmindedly pocketed the card with the telephone number.

As he walked out of the telephone booth he reflected that this had been a full day. Should he simply order a meal—perhaps even in his room in the hotel?—read a book, and go to bed? Tomorrow might be busy. On the other hand as, crossing the river, the evening breeze braced him, he reconsidered: It was more probable that tomorrow would be *un*eventful; that he would be spending the whole of the day or most of it in his room, waiting for instructions. Why not, then, wander about Paris a little bit? Should he call Alouette? Or simply go to the bar at the George V, perhaps run into someone, male or female. Male? "Blacky Oakes! For Pete's sake? Haven't seen you since New Haven. What're you *do*ing?" How many times had that happened to him. One hundred? One thousand? He tried to come up with interesting variations on the theme that he was an international consultant in engineering, in which he was known by all his old classmates to be highly qualified. But, inevitably, there had been rumors. Only once or twice, usually when his friends got drunk—or, more often, when their wives did—the question would be pressed. *Was it true that he was actually in the* . . . By definition, Blackford Oakes was no longer a deep-cover agent. The KGB now knew his identity. But the rules of the Agency were not relaxed. The Agency took the position that even if the Soviet Union discovers the identity of an agent his usefulness in clandestine operations by no means entirely lapses. By staying clear of embassies and U.S. officials in whatever capacity, covert agents retain a measure of mobility. They must constantly be on guard against being followed, because very often they are, and the KGB seems to develop a fascination for the movements of particular agents, for no rational reason. Blackford had been pestered while in Washington, but had eluded the KGB entirely, he was certain, during the months in Budapest, and there was no evidence the KGB were on to him in France. Still, in the middle of a drastically secret operation, he was best off not frequenting a bar, or a restaurant, where he stood a higher chance of running into somebody he knew; so, passing by Au Petit Riche on Rue Le Peletier, he decided impulsively to enter it, and eat alone, and read a little—he carried a pocketbook always, and was enjoying Jane Austen, whom he had once vowed to Sally not to read. "It would embarrass you most awfully, wouldn't it, Dr. Partridge, if after reading Jane Austen it should transpire in conversations in academic salons that I, a mere vulgar engineer, know more about Jane Austen than you do?" She had answered with characteristic vitality that any academic salon which thought that he would ever know more than she about Jane Austen would likely be in Equatorial Guinea. But at the airport he had impetuously picked up *Pride and Prejudice* and, to his amazement, discovered that Jane Austen was most awfully . . . *funny*. So, when the waiter came, he ordered a kir, and a half-dozen snails and a *crêpe de volaille* and a half bottle of Montrachet and later a little cheese and a half bottle of burgundy and then, he decided, Alouette. He rose to the telephone, and she answered immediately.

"Hello, do you speak English?"

"Yess. Who ees thees?"

"Thees ees a friend of Tony's. Do you remember Tony?" He half hoped she would say no.

"Off korss, how ees dear Tonee?"

"He's fine, sends his best. I was wondering whether you would like to go out for a drink?"

"Mmmm. But wy go out? I haf neize champagne right here?"

"Okay. Nine o'clock?"

"It weel be oh so charming to meet a friend of Tonee's."

He went back to the table and, for a minute, felt bad about the forthcoming tryst. But then he reminded himself that Sally had rejected him. All right, more precisely, rejected marriage. What was he to do? There were, of course, austere answers to that question, but he found that with a little discipline, he could drive them from his mind. He returned to his coffee and to Jane Austen, but suddenly he was not focusing. How well he knew the encroaching sensation. Once it began, it directed him, and, worse, he knew it: It was as though he were sitting at the next table, looking at himself. He paid the bill, congratulated the maître d'hôtel, and casually asked for the nearest pharmacy. It was nearby, it happened, and there the transaction—done necessarily through a saleswoman behind the counter, there being no man around—was handled as nonchalantly as if he had asked for a tube of toothpaste. Noting the time, he reasoned he could walk—back across the river, up the Quai Voltaire, past the little hotel where Oscar Wilde had died so wretchedly (but not of venereal disease), and up the Rue du Bac to the indicated number. At worst he would arrive ten minutes late. He set out, the demon now in complete control. He found already that his throat was becoming dry, and he forced himself to look appreciatively at the lights of Paris, which concatenated—was this the special genius of the romantic city?—to shape themselves for him in erotic designs. When he rang the doorbell, he was very nearly hoarse with desire.

Chapter 15

AT FIVE MINUTES to ten Blackford Oakes dropped a coin in the pay phone at the end of the hotel's arcade and dialed Rufus.

"Nothing in *Le Monde*," Rufus began. "I'm not surprised, really. They just haven't decided what to do. A tough question even under serene circumstances. There's a considerable confusion in the Kremlin these days. I see. Perhaps tomorrow. Almost certainly tomorrow. Meanwhile I have some . . . information I want you to take to our friends."

"I should come then by car?"

"Yes, park it nearby."

This was code—and signified that Blackford should park the car at a safe remove from Rufus's apartment and take special care that he was not followed.

"Okay. See you in a bit." Blackford hung up, walked back into the lobby, and notified the cadaverous doorman he wished his car brought up from the garage. He gave him the stub and three hundred-franc bills.

He idled for a few minutes, looking at the morning paper's headlines and lead stories. He had not understood Rufus's reference to the Kremlin—until he read the news of Khrushchev's palace coup. Malenkov, one story reported, was being dispatched to manage a hydroelectric plant in Ust-Kamenogorsk in East Kazakhstan. Blackford made a mental note to be sure to call on Malenkov the next time he was in East Kazakhstan. The Kremlin reported that there would be "no prosecutions" of the dissidents, thus exposing, as *Pravda* had put it, "myths being spread by some Western journalists about the persecution of the members of the antiparty group." Blackford wondered whether Malenkov had been offered as an alternative to Ust-Kamenogorsk the chance of being shot. The doorman approached him. "Monsieur, your car."

He walked around to the driver's seat, slid the car into gear, and turned right down the Rue St.-Honoré. As ever, he looked hard at the rearview mirror, and so he saw the gray Fiat pull out, heading in the same direction. He slowed down long enough to catch the first couple of letters of the license plate, "AJ." He would remember AJ, at least for a little while, in case it came in handy. It was then that he heard the voice speaking in accented but perfectly fluent English.

"I have a .38 revolver pointed at your neck. Head straight the way you're going, into the Rivoli. Close your window. Do exactly as I say or else I shall blow your brains out."

Blackford proceeded through the heavy traffic and attempted through the rearview mirror to look behind him. He couldn't see a head or a torso, but he could see a gloved-hand gripping a revolver aimed directly at the back of his head. His heart was beating rapidly and he felt moisture on his brow.

"Who are you?" He affected a kind of clinical curiosity.

"We will talk later—if you are alive later."

"Why do you say, 'if I am alive later'?"

"Because if we are stopped; or if you have an 'accident'; or if the car goes out of control, I shall shoot you—and there will be no opportunity to talk later."

"I see. You are telling me to drive carefully."

"If you wish to stay alive."

"Where are we going?"

"To where I direct you."

Blackford now knew the national origin of the back-seat driver.

"You're from Hungary. What do you want from me?"

"I said we would *talk later,* and that is the last thing I shall say except to give you instructions. Do you know the turn to Fontainebleau?"

"Which one?"

"Past Place d'Italie."

"Yes."

"Take it."

Blackford looked again in the mirror. A gray Fiat was behind him. He attempted to read the initials but it was behind him by a hundred yards and he didn't dare slow down.

His mind raced. If he had been followed ever since arriving in Paris, then they—whoever the Hungarian represented—knew about the Château St.-Firmin. Hell, if they had followed him right through the whole bus sequence with Kapitsa, the Russians knew everything. But he was confident he hadn't been followed. Surely if they knew about St.-Firmin, they'd have acted quickly to get Kapitsa back, and Rufus would have got wind of it? *Rufus!* Had it *been* Rufus on the telephone? It was a poor connection. Could it have been an impostor? But if they had eliminated Rufus, and had enticed Blackford to go to Rufus's apartment in order to snatch him, why would they bother with a midmorning, center-of-Paris kidnapping? Blackford felt he must try hard to control his judgment. Think purposively. Challenge assumptions. In the first place, why a Hungarian? Who *was* "they"? Automatically, he reminded himself, one thinks in this business that "they" is the Russians. But the Russians, though they had Hungarian agents, wouldn't very likely be using them in Paris—to pick up an American agent.

"One hundred kilometers per hour, no slower, no faster," the voice behind him said. He pressed down the pedal, and prayed that the French police would not be exercising one of their occasional check stops, because he did not doubt that if this happened the man in the rear would indeed pull the trigger. One bullet would dispose of Oakes. That would leave five for the policeman, not bad odds.

They drove in the summer heat up past Orly onto the two-lane highway, which bore no speed limits. They were fifty kilometers out of Paris and suddenly he found himself, through the mirror, looking straight into the face of a young man of slender countenance, light-haired, with regular features, wearing a light blue shirt, workman's smock, no tie, eyes barely discernible behind the squat eyelids. The man glanced hastily out the rear window, clearly to satisfy himself that his car was following. A few minutes later he said to Blackford, "Slow down. You will turn left about a half a kilometer from here on the country road."

It was a mile and one half from that turnoff that his captor directed him to drive through an unused, open gate. "Go toward that barn." Blackford did so, and at that point the Fiat that had followed them off the highway pulled alongside. He looked at a girl in the front seat, dark, with sad eyes and a pale complexion, her hair austerely arranged. She wore a blouse and light blue cotton skirt, and in the summer heat she was perspiring. Her face was strikingly familiar. On her left was a man equally young, of heavy build, his hair carefully groomed, wearing a light brown, ill-cut suit, a set and grim expression on his face.

"What now?"

"Get out of the car."

Blackford did so, and the driver of the adjacent car drew Blackford's hands behind him and tied them securely with electric cord.

"All right, Harry," the man said eye to eye, pointing to the barn door. "Get in there."

"Harry!" Instantly Blackford knew. Great God Almighty, I'm going to be made to pay for the death of Theophilus Molnar!

The irony tormented him, and he actually feared he would be literally speechless. The girl. Frieda! He had last seen her arm in arm with Theo whom she kissed as he left her to come into the tavern for one of those meetings with Blackford.

He entered the dilapidated barn and stopped. He came close to retching, barely controlling himself. There, hanging over an old beam, the light from the open door casting a broad shaft of light illuminating the bottom third of the line, was a noose.

Chapter 16

IVAN DYAKOV WENT eagerly to the newsstand of the hotel, took out his voucher from his wallet, and—knowing no French—pointed to it, smiling. The old man behind the counter took it, went over to a drawer, shuffled through the packages of developed pictures, and drew out the fattest one.

"*Ça fait sept milles huit cent francs.*"

Dyakov shrugged his shoulders. "*Nyet français.*"

The old man wearily wrote out the figure on a scratch pad, Dyakov pulled some notes from his wallet, clutched the packet, grabbed his briefcase, and trotted out lest he delay the bus. He sat next to Valentin Sapolayev, a tall gaunt bearded theoretician whose attention was undistracted from his work. Sapolayev had groaned with impatience on receiving the news that he would be a member of the scientific delegation traveling to Paris. Once arrived, he participated gladly enough in the scientific exchanges, but he went on the afternoon sight-seeing trips only because he was given no alternative. Now, trapped by the genial Dyakov, he had to sit and look at 128 photographs taken by his chattering colleague. He bore up through the first eight rolls, but after plowing through ten different but indifferent shots of the Eiffel Tower, he put his arm over the other's shoulder and said, "Dear Ivan, I think you are a perfectly wonderful photographer. But I think it is unfair to let me monopolize these. Here"—he picked up the pile on his lap, reached over the back of the chair in front of him, and dropped the lot on the lap of Pyotr Viksne.

Viksne, in his bored, businesslike way, inspected the pictures while behind him Dyakov, with squeals of delight, continued to show more and more pictures to the distraught Sapolayev. Suddenly Viksne stopped and stared at one picture. He leaned back at Dyakov.

"You didn't tell me you took a picture of Kapitsa?"

"You mean after the bus accident?"

"Yes."

"Well," Dyakov chuckled. "Obviously I did, though to tell the truth, I had forgotten. Why? There are lots of pictures of Viktor, of Tamara, of you, of everybody."

"Can I borrow this one for a bit?"

"Certainly. Would you like to borrow any of the others? Perhaps have duplicates made? I am sure Mrs. Viksne would be very grateful."

"No. I have a particular interest in this one."

"Well, don't lose it. I'd like to keep my collection complete."

At the Lycée, Viksne told Academician Nesmayanov that Viksne had been called to the embassy and must miss some of the morning's sessions. That in the (unlikely) event he had not returned by noon, Nesmayanov should escort the delegation back to the hotel, then back to the Lycée for the afternoon session.

Outside he signaled a cab and gave the address of the Soviet Embassy. At the entrance, never mind that he had been to the embassy every day since Monday, and was perfectly well known to the guard at the desk, his papers were carefully inspected before the telephone operator was given his name. Sverdlov's secretary, a bosomy Georgian striding uneasily on high French heels, greeted him perfunctorily. In the elevator, neither of them spoke. At Sverdlov's office, Viksne disregarded the greeting and dropped the photograph on Sverdlov's desk. At first the meaning of it did not register. Suddenly it occurred to Viksne that Sverdlov had probably never seen a picture of Kapitsa.

"That was the kidnapping! *That*"—he pointed to the young, smiling face of the car's driver, caught at the moment he offered a ride to Tamara—"is a picture of the kidnapper."

Without further ado Sverdlov rose, photograph in hand, and the two went to the office of the military attaché and asked the secretary to advise Colonel Bolgin that something important had come up. She came out of Bolgin's office holding the door open.

"What is it?" Bolgin asked.

Viksne snatched the picture from Sverdlov and thrust it at Bolgin. "The kidnapper! Now we have a picture of him! Maybe we can get a lead on who he is, what branch of the FLN he's associated with."

Bolgin took the picture, and reached into his pocket for his powerful reading glasses. He looked at the picture. For a moment Viksne thought Bolgin had stopped breathing. His color was changing as they looked at him. His eyes did not leave the photograph. His head turned up, his eyes were closed, and he said simply, "Oh my God!" He then addressed Viksne. He had to clear his voice to speak. "Return to the delegation. Make no further mention of the picture. Call me at noon. If I am unavailable, call me every half hour until you reach me. Understood?"

"Yes, Colonel." He left the room.

"Sverdlov. Find out if Blackford Oakes is at the France et Choiseul *right now*. Last night I concluded arrangements that make it highly probable that he is *not* at the hotel and will never return to it. But *conceivably* he is there still, in which case disperse three men outside the hotel to follow him wherever he goes. *They are not to lose him on any account*. If they do, I guarantee that they will lose their lives. Call me the instant you find out. Quickly"—he motioned impatiently to the door.

He then took out his address book and, applying the code, hunted up the telephone numbers of József Nady. Pray God he could stop him in time.

He rang the home telephone. He let it ring six times. No answer.

He rang the radio shop. A woman answered. József Nady was not in.

"When do you expect him?"

"Don't know. He called in sick this morning. Maybe later on, maybe tomorrow. If it's an emergency, I have his home telephone number somewhere." She yelled out, *"Jean? Jean! Écoutes, Jean . . ."*

Bolgin tried to recapture her attention over the phone. He shouted, "Madame, madame!" But she was bent on getting Jean. . . .

Bolgin hung up. He bowed his head in thought. He jammed his finger on the bell and his secretary walked in. "I am going to the code room. Will be there for a considerable period. Interrupt me only if Sverdlov advises you he has located our party at the hotel. Understand?"

He went out the door and, eschewing the elevator, bounded down the three flights to the code room.

In the room, alone with his personal code, he paused, and wondered. Already his shirt was soaked through with sweat. Would he survive this one? No question about it, if it had been four years earlier, with the Georgian monster at the helm, this would have been the moment to swallow that pill. Well, not now: tonight, after a good read, and a . . . terminal shot of vodka. The situation in Moscow, now that Khrushchev was fully in charge—no doubt about that—might be confused enough not to react against KGB-Europe with draconian ferocity. But what would be the reaction to this? The phrasing of the communication must be done carefully. It should subtly suggest that Bolgin was a little suspicious right from the beginning. But how? After all the back-and-forth on the matter of the *Chekhov*. Great God, the *Chekhov!* He looked at his watch. It would already be out of the Dardanelles. Perhaps it had already received instructions to head west. No matter. It could always be directed to return . . . but not until Kapitsa was back. Would he come back? For a few minutes the confusion, the variables, the contingencies, almost overwhelmed him. He loosened his tie. How grateful he was that no one else was in the room. His improvisation of the night before, which could mean that Oakes was now dead and could never lead them to Kapitsa, he had fortunately not communicated to anyone. Nor would he. He would pay off József from secret funds, then get rid of him. That would be easy. . . . Normally he would have approached the encoder and batted out, with two fingers, the message directly. But now he took a pencil, and the large pad, and made a draft in heavy block letters.

"HAVE DEVELOPED INCONTROVERTIBLE EVIDENCE THAT SEQUESTRATION OF KAPITSA IS A CIA OPERATION. WE CANNOT KNOW AT THIS POINT WHETHER KAPITSA IS ALIVE"—he thought this a good touch. It suggested the CIA might have bungled the job; suggested Kapitsa might have been tortured to death; suggested Kapitsa might have committed suicide—all of which would greatly distract KGB-MOSCOW. "INASMUCH AS WORD OF CHEKHOV'S DESTINATION

WILL NOT REACH AMERICANS UNTIL TOMORROW WE SHOULD KNOW BY END OF DAY WHETHER KAPITSA IS RETURNED TO US. NEED ADVICE ON THREE MATTERS: (1) SHOULD SEARCH FOR CIA OPERATIVE BLACKFORD OAKES WHOSE LINK TO OPERATION HAS BEEN ESTABLISHED PROCEED EVEN AT RISK OF ALERTING SÛRETÉ TO OUR DESIRE TO CATCH UP WITH HIM: (2) SHOULD WE INVOKE FORMAL HELP FRENCH POLICE PROTESTING KIDNAPPING OF SOVIET NATIONAL: (3) SHOULD SPECIAL ARRANGEMENTS BE MADE TO RETURN KAPITSA TO MOSCOW? ADVISE IMMEDIATELY. IN RE CHEKHOV URGENTLY RECOMMEND NO CONTRADICTORY INSTRUCTIONS BE ISSUED BEFORE KAPITSA RETURNS. AWAITING REPLY."

He read it over. He decided it would help to subordinate himself, and accordingly he changed the phrase "NEED ADVICE" to "REQUEST INSTRUCTIONS." Then he decided he had been too hortatory in the matter of *Chekhov,* and recasted the sentence to begin with the phrase: "I ASSUME YOU WILL NOT CONTRADICT." His code book was in front of him, he transcribed the words, and one half hour later, the message was put on the desk of Gleb Mamulov, new Director General of the KGB, his predecessor having been, in the meantime, shot.

Chapter 17

THE OLD BARN had been a storehouse for wine casks, dozens of them scattered about in varying stages of dilapidation, on the dusty dimly illuminated rotting wooden floor. Erno had traveled out at dawn to loop the rope and contrive a rudimentary courtroom. He found a stout plank which he propped up over two old wine casks—they would sit on the plank. A large barrel would serve József, the chief judge, as a table. Another cask, serving as a bench, would be for the defendant.

To that seat Blackford was now guided. "Sit," József motioned with the pistol. The three Hungarians moved in front of him. They sat down on the plank, the man with the gun in the middle, the girl on his right. The man in the blue shirt placed the pistol on the cask in front of him, the barrel pointing at Blackford. The tool chest József had brought from the car he placed under the plank.

The trial of Harry Browne had begun.

" 'Harry,' as you call yourself, I am József Nady. This is Frieda Darvas—I am aware that you have met her—and on my left is Erno Toth. We are here to try you for conspiring to deliver Theophilus Molnar to Soviet executioners on the seventh of November 1956. Do you plead guilty or not guilty?"

Blackford drew breath and said most solemnly, *"Not guilty."*

"Do you deny that you gave him a key to an address on Dohany Street?"

"No, I don't deny it. It is true that I gave him the key. I sought to protect him. I knew he was likely to get into trouble."

"How could the Soviet executioners have got hold of the address on Dohany Street unless you were in collusion with them?"

"I don't know. I have tortured myself wondering. There is only one explanation. It is that Theo disobeyed my orders and confided the address to someone from whom the Russians got it, possibly by torture."

József turned to his companions and spoke in Hungarian. The tones were unmistakably contemptuous. The girl said nothing, but Erno gestured to József, then addressed Blackford: *"Sprechen sie Deutsch?"*

Yes, said Blackford, he spoke German.

The questioning resumed. What was Oakes's profession?

Blackford thought for a moment, decided he had very little to lose.

"I am an American intelligence agent. I take orders from the CIA."

"In that case," József broke in sneeringly, reverting to English, which Toth evidently understood but had difficulty in speaking, "you should be able to prove you are with the CIA. What were you doing in Budapest?"

"I was collecting information for the Agency on the likelihood of a revolt against the puppet government, and the probable popular reaction to such a revolt. In addition, I had a hand in establishing contact points for escape routes."

"Oh? Where did you establish these contact points?"

Blackford was at once eager to convince, and wary.

"Some of those I helped to establish have been detected. One or two, so far as I know, continue to operate."

"But where *were* these contact points?"

"You must realize that you are asking me for information I am under no circumstances permitted to give out. There are lives at stake."

"Including your own," said József, looking up at the noose.

Blackford decided to take a risk. A reasonable risk. He turned to Frieda. "You came out through the candy store of Madame Zlaty on Ferenc Street."

Frieda was visibly startled.

József on the other hand was triumphant. "Ah! And three days later Madame Zlaty was arrested, tortured, and executed!"

Blackford's face reddened, and he lost his temper. "You're saying I set up that old lady to get tortured and shot? Fuck you, Nady. If the revolution was made up of types like you, I'm glad you lost!"

The effect of Blackford's outburst was convulsive. All three Hungarians spoke at the same time. József kept gesturing toward the hangman's rope. Erno appeared to wish to pursue the interrogation. Frieda, after an initial burst, left it to the men to contend with each other, but appeared to detach herself from them. Suddenly there was silence. József spoke:

"What are you doing in Paris, Oakes?"

Blackford was startled to hear his own name, which he had never used, in Budapest or in Paris. The others did not appear to have noticed an obtrusive syllable. Blackford let it go.

"I am here to pick up whatever information my superiors ask me for."

"What have they asked you to look into?"

"I am not on assignment at the moment."

József spat on the floor to give conviction to *his* disbelief. He conversed now with Erno, who nodded his head as he spoke. Frieda listened, and then addressed Blackford quietly. "Do you wish to pray?"

He broke into heavy sweat. "Yes," he managed to say, and closed his eyes. The talking had stopped, and the three judges were on their feet.

Blackford, pale, opened his eyes and addressed Frieda. "I wish to talk to you alone."

József gestured his refusal impatiently.

But Frieda turned on József angrily, and pushing him to one side stepped forward, took Oakes firmly by the arm, and led him away a few steps to the corner of the barn. She whispered, "What do you want to say to me?"

"That I loved Theo. That when he was killed, which was done before my eyes, I came close to going mad. That because he died, I renewed my pledge to devote my life to avenging him and others who suffer every day from similar fates. I wanted you to know that I too have a fiancée I love, as you loved Theo. She is an American. She was going to marry me as soon as I left the Agency. She broke off the engagement *because I refused to leave after seeing Theo killed.* And then I wanted to tell you one more thing."

Frieda stepped back for one moment, shaken. She saw Blackford, his face white, the sweat of his agony suppurating through his shirt, his hands bound behind him. Theo must have looked much like that in those final moments. In her mind's eye she saw them together, Theo and Blackford, and she recalled, in a way she had entirely forgotten, the communion between the two men. Could such a man have betrayed Theo?

"What was it you wanted to add?"

Blackford's whisper was hoarse: It was now, or never, he knew.

"That I arranged with a bank in Paris to advise the fiancée of Theophilus Molnar that Theophilus's aunt had turned over a part of her savings to that bank and directed that the money should be paid to Frieda Darvas. That bank made inquiries and tracked you down. The money was in fact my own money. The Crédit Lyonnais acted on my instructions. Theophilus was betrayed, yes. But not by me."

She stared at him, ashen. Tears began to flow. She reached out her hand, forgetting that he could not take it. Then Frieda clenched her teeth, and turned to her partners.

They spoke interminably, the pitch of their voices rising to a yell. But Blackford could see that Erno was apparently now arguing with Frieda, not against her. At one point Erno left the little group, came over to Oakes, wheeled him about, and untied the line holding his wrists together. Oakes spotted a movement by József and lunged across the room, hitting him with a tackle seconds before József's hand reached the pistol on the wine cask. They struggled furiously. Oakes smashed him, using the bottom of his hand with all his force on the bridge of the nose, stepping to one side as József fell, and then kicked him hard on the temple, leaving him motionless. Breathing heavily, Blackford turned to the girl and Erno. There was an interval before he could speak.

"There is your traitor."

Frieda and Erno talked hoarsely in Hungarian. Blackford interrupted them. "How did József know Theo had a hiding place on Dohany Street?"

Erno replied. "He told us that Theo said you had given him a hiding place on the street but that Theo hadn't given him the number."

"I should have known," Frieda said, as if to herself. "If Theo had a hiding place, he would never keep it merely for himself. He would never give out the street to a friend, and not give the address. He and József were together at the field house when the Russians came. He must have told him then." She looked at Blackford directly. "I believe you." And to Erno she said, "Our colleague," spitting it out at the figure on the floor, "is Theo's killer."

The rays of the sun, risen to its meridian, had left them in relative darkness. "Is he dead?" Erno asked Oakes.

"I expect he is." He got down on his knees, and put his fingers on József's wrist.

"Yes."

Again there was silence. Frieda finally spoke. "We'll have to bury him, Harry; can you attend to that?"

"I'll see to it. And quickly. It is now clear József was on assignment today."

"What do you mean?"

Blackford reached into the tool kit and opened it inquisitively. Along with the paraphernalia of a radio repairman was a black object with a circular aluminum attachment. He drew it out. "József was going to take a picture of me—hanging from that beam. I assume he was in touch with people who would have paid him well for the picture."

Frieda came to him, and extended her hand. Blackford impulsively put his arms about her. They walked silently to the cars.

Chapter 18

BLACKFORD OAKES was at an apartment on Avenue du Roule in Neuilly. The kitchen was well stocked. Impatiently he opened a bottle of red wine, took out a tin of crackers, and chewed absentmindedly, without appetite. Two hours earlier, from the outskirts of Paris, he had telephoned Rufus.

"I'm hot."

Rufus's voice did not change. Indeed it was unchangeable. "I see. Can you meet me at Adam's house in twenty minutes?"

Adam's house was emergency meeting point #1, even as Baker's house was emergency meeting point #2.

Number one was at the Louvre, in the Salle Mollien; they sat in the fauteuil looking at canvases by David.

"They're on to me. Tried to kill me, using a double agent from the Hungarian freedom-fighting gang. He's dead and I've drawn a map giving the exact location of the barn where the body is, about fifty kilometers out on the road to Fontainebleau. Can you take care of that?"

"Yes . . . maybe even with due ceremony. Go on." Blackford slipped Rufus a rolled newspaper.

"Okay, next problem. They tracked me from the hotel. So I can't go back there. Somebody's going to have to collect my gear right away and check me out. Better than just leaving it there, do you agree?"

"I'm not so sure. Your room is probably being watched. If we pick up your stuff, we'll have to shake them off. Besides, they'd guess then that their mission didn't succeed."

"They'll know that when Nady fails to show up with the photograph. Fails to show at all."

"Yes. But he wouldn't necessarily be expected to show up right away. We'd confuse them for a while anyway. At any rate, give me your room key and the key to your car. We'll have to dispose of that. I know where it's parked. I was watching. How many were involved?"

"There were three of them; the other two are good guys. One's a girl. I'll give you the details later. Where do I go?"

"To the Avenue du Roule in Neuilly. Ring the bell and tell the landlady Madame Rondpoint told you to use her apartment. She'll let you into 4D and give you a room key. Don't move until you hear from me. The place was swept a week ago and the telephone is clear. From now on use a disguise. A beret, a pair of glasses. Give me your sunglasses, and I'll have a plain-glass pair made up and sent to the apartment along with the hat."

Blackford drew breath, and felt free to ask:

"How's it going at Chantilly?"

"Very good. I made other arrangements to get the material to Trust when you didn't show up this morning. Tell me the name of the dead man. You said 'Nady'? We'll try to get a line on him."

"It's written on the map. Phonetically—I forgot to get the spelling from the girl."

"Do you know how to contact her?"

"I know a bank that has her address."

"If they tracked you beginning Monday, they'd have moved in on the operation by now. My guess is they didn't pick up your trail until yesterday. What perplexes me is why they would want to bump you off when you might have led them to Kapitsa." Rufus paused. Oh God, thought Blackford: He is going into one of those infuriating trances. Of all times.

But it didn't last long. Rufus said, "I shall do some thinking. You'll hear from me. Some clothes and toiletries will be delivered to the landlady." Rufus rose, and ambled leisurely down the gallery, pausing here and there to consult the catalogue he had bought at the ticket office. Blackford walked down the staircase, past the "Winged Victory," and stepped into a taxi. He directed the driver to take him to the public gymnasium at the Hôtel Claridge on the Champs-Élysées. There he got out, paid the thousand-franc locker fee, picked up a towel, and went up to the second floor. For an hour he worked out, running through every exercise he knew as vigorously as he could, using the punching bag and the bicycle and the rowing machine and throwing himself, finally, into the large green pool with the sickly-tepid water. He showered and, his towel wrapped around him, closed his eyes as he lay on one of the gymnasium reclining mattresses; but he didn't sleep. It was enough that he didn't dream. After a half hour he rose, approached the locker, oblivious of the two attendants in the otherwise empty gym who, though it was their routine business to witness exertion, remarked that his had been a most extraordinary example of it.

"*Tiens*," said the fat man in his clinical white. "*Avec raison il garde sa ligne.*" (No wonder he's so trim.) Blackford dropped a five-hundred-franc note in the wicker basket, nodded *merci*, and went out.

* * *

Halfway through the second cracker and after the first glass of wine, he realized that he had suddenly become hungry. He explored the refrigerator. There was chicken, ham, cheese, white wine. He put together a plate with slabs of each and, after finishing the red wine, opened the white. He drew up his chair to the kitchen table and suddenly felt an eerie sense of joy. He could not exactly situate it in the repertory of his emotions. He had been a combat pilot in the last days of the war, and knew what it was to emerge the victor in a dogfight. Was it the same feeling? No, it was, somehow, far deeper. He felt almost like laughing. He drank another glass of wine and put more salt on the chicken. Was there a radio? He would like to hear music. In the salon he found an ancient set which, however, worked; and brought him a Frenchman who droned on for a bit, but whose voice gave way finally to the overture to *Don Giovanni*. He opened the drawer of the desk, found writing paper, and sat down.

> Dear Sally:
> And what did *you* do today? I of course miss you, and continue to wonder why it is that you insist that I

resign my placid career in order to practice engineering in Washington, D.C., while you teach the Georgian novel to that little band, those happy few, who are left hungry after feasting on the cornucopia of twentieth-century literature. What would you like me to build for you? Tell me. *Anything.* Sky's the limit. Skyscraper you say? Where would you like it, and how tall? Will you order the cement for me, and have it ready when I come back? Since my leave may be for only two or three weeks, I wouldn't want to waste any time. Let me see. I should think 28 stories would be about right, one for every year you have graced. Order me 180,000 tons of cement, 80 miles of nickel steel beams—I'll leave it to you to specify the size, that way it will be your-and-my skyscraper. Figure 5 bathrooms per story, times 28, 140. One hundred and forty toilets, washstands, tubs, showers—bidets? I leave that to you. Twelve acres of carpet—my Sally will have wall-to-wall. When Blacky does things, *he does them wall-to-wall.* Decorations? I have taken a liking to Miró. Please order 140 Mirós—do you want his address? I'll give you a secret telephone number in Washington where you can get unlisted phone numbers, SPo-okie. Easier to remember than numbers. Did you ask me am I drunk? I resemble that. I have to confess something. I told somebody today I was "devoting" my life to resisting the tyrants. I'm ashamed of myself. It made me sound pompous. I'd rather die than sound pompous. Actually, that's not true. I'd rather sound pompous than die. Oh dear how I miss you. It has been a hectic day. More in a couple of days,

Love,
Blacky

He scratched out the address on an envelope, sealed it, and was wondering why in the hell he hadn't heard from Rufus when the phone rang.

"Everything all right?"

"Yeah. Don Giovanni just finished screwing another nympho."

"I want you with the others. Anthony will explain. He will pick you up at six in the morning. Your belongings will be in his car. We'll talk tomorrow."

"Okay, Rufus. Say, I feel like gambling. Thought I'd go to the races at the Bois de Boulogne tomorrow. Want to come?"

"Good night."

"Good night."

Chapter 19

BLACKFORD ROSE AT five-thirty, put water on the stove, and, impatient to discover which switch corresponded with which burner, flicked all six of them on. He went to the window and instinctively shielded himself from view while peering out at an angle. It was raining heavily and the air was warm, the light still meager. His baggage consisted of *Pride and Prejudice,* which he stuck in his pocket, the few toilet articles he had found in the paper bag on the bed, the beret, and the glasses. Opening the door, he locked it behind him after spotting Trust pulling up outside. He dropped the key in the landlady's mailbox and bounded out, opening the car door and sliding into the right seat.

Trust slipped the little Mercedes 180 into gear.

"Let's stop at a newsstand. Or have you already looked?"

"No, too early. There's one at the Porte Champerret. You had a rough day. I see it affected your eyesight."

"Yeah. I figured it all out. I was paying for the evening before."

"Ah so. Did I exaggerate?"

"Anthony, you only exaggerate when you recruit people into this goddam Agency."

"Here, take the umbrella." Trust reached to the back seat as he braked. Blackford dashed out. Trust saw him gesticulating to the vendor impatiently. He finally returned with a copy of *Le Monde*.

"What's the trouble?"

"The old goat wanted to see me some feelthy pictures."

"Are they out already?"

"Are what out already?"

"The pictures of you and Alouette?"

"Fun-nee." Blackford was flipping the pages of the bulky daily while Trust groped his way to the turnoff at Porte de Clignancourt. He came to the personals and ran his finger down the columns. "Here it is!" He read it haltingly, translating as he went. "'To Anna Krupskaya. I think you are . . . *te portes*—behaving very . . . unreasonably. I have always been . . . faithful to you and your ideals. The specific . . . *prière*—demand? . . . the specific demand you have made is acceptable but the articles cannot be *livrés*—delivered . . . until we are reunited. Immediately after that the distribution will be made. I am your brother.'"

"That's all?"

"Yeah. They want Kapitsa back before the *Chekhov* puts in at Bizerte. Not a bad situation from our point of view. We can just haggle."

"Rufus doesn't like to draw out these situations. In the first place, that note isn't very different from what they'd place there if they were on our track. They'd want to stall, just as we want to stall. Well, it's up to Rufus, but he'll want an update on the St.-Firmin situation."

"That's what I want, too," said Blackford. "That and a breakfast roll." Trust stopped by a bakery and again Blackford popped out, returning with a two-foot loaf of French bread and two bottles of Coca-Cola.

"Ugh," said Trust, accepting both gratefully, wedging the cold bottle between his knees, and taking a bite from the hunk of bread Blackford gave him.

"Okay, buddy, talk."

Trust slowed down to avoid a great big wet shaggy dog being chased by a distraught woman pulling an open umbrella behind her. He swallowed his mouthful and extended his hand for another piece of bread.

"They've been together now for almost two days. Beginning yesterday, I spent time with them—Tamara, by the way, speaks perfect English, and Kapitsa's isn't bad, so there isn't any trouble communicating, though of course they slide into Russian all the time. We're 'friends' of Vadim from America. Vadim told us about Kapitsa when he found out reading the Russian press that his old Vorkuta camp-mate would be a member of the scientific delegation going to Paris for the International Geophysical Year bit. Vadim came to us—you're an engineer, doing collateral work for the Air Force in the area of Cocoa Beach, where the launchers are, and you're pretty savvy about rockets—though don't worry, no specific ignorance will surprise Viktor. I'm an international lawyer, an old friend of yours. Our friend in Paris—Rufus—is a retired intelligence officer. We acted on our own. If he decides he wants to defect, we'll tell him the real story; tell him we began by deceiving him—for his own protection."

"Does he *want* to defect?"

"I don't think so. My feeling is he would like to get away from a system he loathes—Vadim told me, after they had gone to bed last night, that Viktor's old rage, suppressed for four years, burst out this morning, and in front of Tamara—apparently they don't talk about it between themselves. But he seems to be terribly afraid to do anything decisive. Tamara is taking a pretty straightforward position: She'll do anything he wants. But my guess is she is calculating one thing only."

"Viktor?"

"Viktor. She told Vadim, when they were alone in the kitchen, that on the one hand she liked the idea of going to America, where Viktor would be safe from the kind of caprice that put him in Vorkuta, but that on the other hand, he is sitting now with so much high-powered information about the state of the Soviet art in rockets she wonders whether they wouldn't succeed in tracking him down wherever he was, and bumping him off. She's also very concerned about the Algerian business. Concerned whether the cover will stand up if Viktor decides to go back to Russia."

"Have you gotten anywhere trying to reassure her?"

"Vadim has been great. He told Viktor that if he decides to pull out of Russia, Vadim knows how to put him in the hands of the CIA. Then he described to Viktor the kind of care that the Agency has taken of him in the past few years, stressing that in America he and Tamara would be physically safe. That was part good, part bad—because Viktor said he would have to continue his work if he went to the U.S., that he couldn't just rusticate. He's terribly involved, intellectually and emotionally, in the satellite launch—as we know. And Vadim, who obviously talks the scientific lingo with perfect facility, hasn't had any trouble at all in drawing Viktor out. Vadim is writing down at night everything Viktor tells him, and Rufus is coding it all to Washington and Von Braun, and we've already got back a terrific lot of questions to ask based on leads he's given us. It's fascinating to listen to him, Vadim told me last night. The security neurosis in that ghetto they live in at Tyura Tam has got to be suffocating; so he's getting a tremendous kick out of telling Vadim, scientist to scientist, the problems they've faced, the problems they've cracked, the kind of talk, he says, he can't feel free to have even with his own colleagues. He says he's working—like the rest of them—day and night under breakneck pressure; he says Khrushchev wants the thing up so bad he can taste it. But—get this!—he told Vadim *nothing* would delight Viktor—and Tamara!—personally more than if we got ours up before theirs."

"Hey man!" Blackford found the report exhilarating. He asked then the critical question: "Are they pretty close to going?"

"That's the good part. Answer: No. They've got a problem, something to do with the circuits in the satellite and the need to pack more power into the transistors. They're trying everything. I have a feeling they could get a dispensation to go to the Vatican to pray to St. Jude. They're going crazy—but they haven't got it licked. They've got the launch, Viktor says, but not the electronic staying power. And they don't want to send a lemon up there."

"Do we have the same problem?"

"Apparently not." Anthony Trust brought the Mercedes practically to a standstill to peer through the rain and see if he had reached the turn to the chateau. "We've got a problem with the launching fuel, and Viktor has given Vadim a couple of leads the Washington people want pursued. That's what I have to tell Vadim—giving specific questions—first thing this morning."

"Why did Rufus decide to pull me in from Paris?"

"If they decide to defect, Rufus had decided they should go separately. You would be escorting the girl. Vadim and I would take Kapitsa. Rufus wants you to—I quote him, God bless his . . . say, Blacky, is it possible Rufus is an illegitimate son of Queen Victoria? Courtesy of that Scottish guy? I mean, one-half Victoria and one-half a randy gamekeeper, *that's Rufus*—Rufus wants you to 'gain their confidence'—his words. That will be interesting. Tamara is something, let me tell you."

"You don't have to. I could see that in the taxi, though we didn't speak in English."

It was seven-fifteen, and the rain had intensified. The road to the chateau had become muddy. Anthony slowed down. He drove the car into the garage, acknowledging the friendly gesture from the well-concealed security guard at the caretakers' cottage, whose radio had been tuned to activate anything from a single helicopter to a marine unit. Anthony thrust the umbrella into Blackford's hand and sprinted across the courtyard into the chateau. Blackford followed him at a lope, and walked through the door Trust was holding open. He followed Trust into the servants' parlor by the kitchen. There Vadim was sitting, absentmindedly stirring his coffee. He greeted Oakes.

Without going into detail, Anthony had passed along to Vadim word of Oakes's ordeal (at Rufus's instruction); and instinctively Vadim felt toward Blackford that protectiveness he felt for everyone who had suffered, or risked suffering, at the hands of the same people who had sustained Vorkuta. Vadim said nothing, but Blackford felt a special warmth in his handshake.

Trust tore out the clipping from *Le Monde* and handed it to Vadim. "Black, why don't you go upstairs and call Rufus—he'll have seen the paper by now. I'm going to talk Vadim through the inquiries that came in from Washington."

Taking his coffee with him, Blackford climbed the stairs and rang Rufus. Blackford thought he detected a note of excitement in Rufus's voice, but he dismissed the notion as intrinsically inconceivable.

"Good morning. The reply to our friends should be dispatched by someone other than yourself, given the events of yesterday, the odd bits and pieces of which have by the way been disposed of." Good old Rufus, Blackford thought, not even sarcastically. "I have been receiving considerable traffic from our principals and the decision is to try for Option #3. If he consents, the mechanical arrangements have already been worked out on a contingency basis, and you will instruct him after getting the details from me. We are thinking in terms of getting a final decision from him tonight. Spend the day with him and with her. The tack is that Option #3 permits them to have it both ways. He gets to work at home on his own thing, but also serves the higher cause. Do you understand me well enough to communicate completely with Vadim?"

"Yes. What is the timetable if he goes along?"

"That will depend. We are making inquiries. If in fact the vessel is headed west, then our representations are being accepted. In that event we can move more deliberately. Otherwise we may need a quick movement."

"When will you know?"

"By early afternoon, though it depends a little on the weather."

"I got you. Am I to call?"

"No. I'll call." Rufus hung up. Blackford went downstairs into the little parlor and shut the door behind him. He remained standing.

"Instructions from Rufus: We are to attempt to persuade Viktor to go back to Russia and pass us information on a regular basis. The most secure conceivable arrangements have been worked out on a standby basis. The line is the obvious one: He can help the cause of freedom, while continuing his own work in his own country surrounded by his own friends. Vadim is to make the decision whether the proposition should be put to him alone, or jointly to Viktor and Tamara. If possible we want an answer, or in any event an indication of what the answer is likely to be, by tonight. Our response to the Soviets on the Algerian matter will depend on whether our aerial reconnaissance reveals that in fact the *Chekhov* is headed toward Tunisia. If it is, then they have swallowed our story and we're safe for the time being. If not, then there are several possibilities, among them that they have a lead on us."

"At which point? . . ." Trust asked.

"At which point, as ever, we will do whatever Rufus tells us to do."

Chapter 20

BLACKFORD WAS ASTONISHED at the informality of Viktor Kapitsa and Tamara when he was introduced to them by Vadim. The couple had breakfasted as usual in the sitting room by their bedroom, read the papers and, gluttonously, assorted journals to which, in Russia, they had no access. It was ten-thirty and the weather had suddenly cleared, the sun turned bright, and the air, ventilating the main living room on the ground floor with a cross draft, was fresh and sweet, and a little of the languor of summer crept in, with the scent from the rose garden. On the little lake the swans were parading; there was a rowboat up on the grass, and stillness.

Tamara's face brightened. "Well, our taxi driver!" Vadim gave Blackford's name as "Julian Booth."

"I am delighted to meet you formally, Mr. Booth, notwithstanding that your detour to our hotel has proved longer than you gave us any idea it would be."

Blackford smiled, shook her hand, and then the hand of the tall, thoughtful, gentle Viktor.

"I'm sorry about that, Madame Kapitsa—"

"Tamara."

"Thank you. I'm Julian. But I'm especially glad you and Dr. Kapitsa are getting a little relaxation."

Tamara looked at Vadim. "It has been a great pleasure to come to know the man who saved my husband's life, and who has remained through all these years his best friend." She spoke matter-of-factly, but there was a flighty femininity in her tones Blackford had difficulty in reconciling with her reputation as an established astrophysicist. She wore a summer dress of vivid pink with a white silk sash and deep V-neck. Vadim had sought expert advice on a modest but chic wardrobe for the unexpected guests, freshly arrived from drabness. She had her own small pearl necklace her husband had purchased on the black market with money earned by tutoring the son of a high Soviet bureaucrat who sought admission into the Lenin Institute of Technology. She wore it always, except when at work. That, and a little gold band on her wedding finger, were all the jewelry she owned. Viktor wore light flannel gray slacks and moccasins, a blue shirt, and a very light sweater. He looked strangely at ease. Clearly he was overjoyed that Tamara shared his fondness for Vadim, who now was acting the role of the constantly solicitous host. The telephone rang and the maid summoned "Monsieur Booth." Blackford climbed the stairs, and was back in two minutes.

"Hot dog! The *Chekhov* is headed toward Tunisia. There now, Dr. Kapitsa—"

"Viktor."

"There now, Viktor, that suggests the esteem in which you are held by your patrons in the Kremlin."

"I prefer to think of them as my owners."

Tamara winced. Viktor was openly violating his pledge never to express himself politically. But the news clearly elated her, and she spoke in rapid Russian to Viktor, while Vadim nodded his head in agreement, and then Vadim turned to Blackford. "I agree. I agree. It is now practically not conceivable that they doubt the Algerian cover story. Not conceivable." And then, in a subdued voice the Kapitsas, who continued talking to each other, could not hear, Vadim asked quietly, "Does Rufus say what message he is going to give back to the embassy?"

"No. Except he said that whatever the reply he finally decides on, he wants to deliver it in time for tomorrow's *Le Monde*. I'm set to go to work on Tamara, but it would be better if you suggested the outing."

Vadim turned and put his arm over Viktor's shoulder. "Quiet! Quiet, everybody, and listen to Uncle Vadim. I need to stay with Viktor for several hours to speak with him. Tamara, you have earned a little relax. I am quite certain that the French police do not look for you. Quite certain there is not given a general alert. I think Julian here can, without running any risk, take Tamara out to visit Chantilly, and perhaps have lunch—he tells me he has a favorite restaurant here. Anthony can stay in to keep up communications with Paris. All is clear?"

Tamara addressed her husband in Russian. He replied briefly. Only then did she say, "Yes, I should be very happy to do a little touring with you, Julian. Thank you."

She had been once to Leningrad, she told him as they left the car in the parking lot and approached the warm chateau, surrounded by water from which summer mists rose like vapor on that windless day. And over there, she explained, the reconstruction of the old czarist palaces was progressing nicely. "Except for the palace at Tsarskoye Selo where Alexandra and the last Czar lived," she chatted. "That is in disrepair. There was only a single foot soldier there, to shoo people away. The Bolshevik mind is *so* inscrutable. It is all right to restore all the beauty of the fabulous gardens of Peter's summer palace, all the fanatical opulence of Catherine's palace—that doesn't offend them historically. But they do not wish to draw attention to the last, relatively modest, chateau of the last Czar. Do you know what I think?"

Her animation surprised Blackford. Why had he supposed that a Russian physicist, if she happened to be beautiful, should compensate by being dull? "No," he said, as he took her arm to help her slide through the narrow ticket entrance, "what do you think?"

"I think the Soviet leadership isn't really comfortable with the concept of regicide. It could, after all, happen to them. Stalin was morbidly paranoiac. He had good reason to be. I would suppose that any time during the thirties until the end, if you had sentenced him to death and asked for an executioner you'd have had about fifty million volunteers."

"One to represent each person he was responsible for killing?"

"I suppose the figures vaguely correspond. But the business of Nicholas and Alexandra is fascinating. The authorities feel it is necessary to stress and re-stress the evil of the last Czar, though they don't much bother in the history books, or on the museum tours, to stress the evils of their predecessors, whose palaces are maintained as museums. More, really, than museums. They are very nearly treated as shrines. But not that poor palace where poor stupid Nicholas spent those weeks before the long journey to Ekaterinburg, and where his guards amused themselves by tripping up his bicycle when he exercised. Now look at this." She waved her hand in an arc pointing to the sumptuous and stately Chantilly: "It's grander, I would say, than the Czar's last palace."

"Wait a minute," Blackford objected. "Nicholas lived there *only* because he happened to like it. Whenever he felt like it, he could hunker down at the Winter Palace. And this whole thing could fit in one of the wings of that palace."

"Yes, the Czars treated themselves with much generosity." Her eyes twinkled, and Blackford marveled that such spontaneity could flower in the parched earth of Soviet society. He decided, as they strolled down the manicured gardens, to say so:

"Tamara, you speak as if you had never worn a straitjacket."

"It isn't the scientists in the Soviet Union who suffer systematic repression. Political repression, of course. But certain modes of freedom are necessary to scientific success."

"Tell that to the critics of Lysenko."

"Lysenko engaged in a science that impinges on ideology. Viktor and I do not. How to launch a satellite is an instrumental, not an ideological, problem. In our own milieu we are much freer than the poets, or the painters, or even the musicians."

"Free to discuss nonscientific matters?"

"Of course not, as I say. Our opinions are private, and there is a great deal of complacency, resignation, fatalism. Even some optimism. Scientists aren't men of affairs. You have an American who wrote 'Scientists are people who build the Brooklyn Bridge and then buy it.'"

"Where did you hear *that?*"

"I forget. We are permitted to read the foreign technical journals. Some of them are quite funny sometimes, especially in the letters' section. Anyway," she went on, "our scientists are working for Stalin's Russia because they are not permitted to give thought to what they do—and because they don't want to. The great Sakharov gave the Kremlin a hydrogen bomb. Why?"

"Why are you about to give them a satellite?"

"Because a scientist develops his own momentum. It is . . ." she looked at him with an expression entirely clinical on her open face, "sexual, in a way: The excitement begins, consummation is required. Viktor—is there anyone in the world who feels more keenly than he does the suffering of the Russian people? It would be hard to name anyone; but he . . . works."

"Why criticize Sakharov?"

"Sakharov succumbed to scientific hubris when he gave the bomb to the Kremlin. But who knows?" She furrowed her brow. "Most creative men who set out to create, and are permitted to do so, will do their utmost. You are familiar with the Church of St. Basil commissioned by Ivan the Terrible? The paintings done for the Borgias? The rockets built for Hitler? By the same man, incidentally, who is at this very moment trying to improve on them for the same man—Eisenhower—who led the army that beat Hitler."

As they spoke, they looked at the Sèvres collection. "Those," said Tamara, "were assembled for the successor to the French King whose motto at Versailles is that he 'Governs by Himself.' Our Russian 'autocrat,' the Czar, reached out for a Greek, not a Slavic term to describe the full scope of his powers. Which reminds me, what are you by profession?"

"I am an engineer."

She paused, and looked up at Blackford, square in the eye.

"What is a cantilever truss?"

Blackford raised his eyebrows, and paused, a smile bursting to come out: "It's a horizontal span supported in the middle and sustaining loads at either end—sort of like bras." He pursed his lips professionally.

She smiled, a radiant smile.

"Are you here in France to build bridges?" she asked.

"That's one way to put it."

"How long really have you known Vadim?"

They were back in the car now, driving slowly toward Café Tipperary. Blackford found himself furiously resentful at the necessary lie. "Since shortly after he came to America."

"How did you come to meet him?"

"He lectured one day at the home of Countess Tolstoi. A friend invited me there. We have been in touch ever since." The cover story had been rehearsed. He wondered whether she had asked Vadim the identical question.

"Do you know what I think?"

"No," he lied.

"I think you are an American intelligence agent."

He laughed.

"Why do you laugh?"

"Because women have a marvelous faculty for making conversation unprofitable. Whatever I say will leave you suspicious."

"I have no objections to American intelligence agents. I have very great objections to anyone hurting my Viktor. If only you knew Viktor! He is, to begin with, a genius. But he is—so special, so loving, so patient. You will never do anything to hurt him?"

"*I* certainly will never do anything to hurt him." Blackford felt he was entitled to say that much. But he felt a twinge in the stomach. He thought of Theo.

What the hell. He was a professional. He had better recapture the offensive. He said: "Would *you* do anything to hurt Viktor?"

"Why do you ask me that?" She seemed both startled and offended.

"Suppose he tells Vadim he wishes to cooperate with the West?"

"*He has already done that*. He spoke half the day yesterday about the scientific work we are doing at Tyura Tam."

"I mean, suppose he told Vadim he wanted to help the West even while living and working in the Soviet Union?"

"I would not permit it. Because there is no safe way to do this."

"There is no truly safe way to do anything in your country. Viktor knew that even before he went to Vorkuta."

"Julian, you are being quite silly. It is true it isn't *safe* for *anyone* to live in the Soviet Union. But it is a *lot* safer to live in the Soviet Union if you are *not* a spy for the United States."

"You are speaking entirely of physical safety. I asked you if you would ever do anything to *hurt* Viktor. Suppose it made him a happier man to contribute to the cause of freedom even at some risk to himself?" Blackford wondered whether the CIA had unconsciously taught him scholastic argumentation or whether he was naturally cursed with the talent.

Tamara fell silent. They got out of the car and walked across the street to the restaurant, which was half empty. Blackford ordered a bottle of Musigny while she looked absentmindedly at the simple menu.

"Could I give you some advice?"

"About what?" she snapped.

"About the menu, Tamara."

With a clearly synthetic gesture of impatience she flung the menu to one side. "If you are going to run my life, you may as well order my meals." Then she smiled at him, but there was concern on her face, and she ate lightly and distractedly from the wonderful dishes placed in front of her, and Blackford, emphatically, left uneaten one-half what he was served. The conversation was about life in America.

Chapter 21

TRUST WAS WAITING for them when they reached St.-Firmin. He smiled at Tamara and told her Vadim and Viktor were out walking. She said she would go to her room and rest, thanked Blackford distractedly, and climbed the staircase.

"You're to call Rufus. I haven't had a chance to quiz Vadim, but I gather things are going well. Any difficulty"—he pointed discreetly toward the staircase—"with her?"

"Yup. She's on to us."

Trust whistled.

"When you think of it, it doesn't make that much difference—unless Viktor should feel betrayed, and that's unlikely, given his attitude. After all, we're not forcing him to do anything. If he wants us to escort him to the U.S. and leave him alone, we'll do that. Tamara's not resentful, she's just afraid. I'll ring Rufus."

Rufus told Blackford to come to Paris at about 11 P.M., driving Trust's car. "We'll meet at Mme. Rondpoint's. Contrive to talk to Serge just before leaving. We'll want the latest on the state of mind of our friend. Anything for me?"

"I had a few hours with the girl. Nothing that won't hold until I see you later." Rufus hung up. Blackford told Trust it looked like a late evening, so he might as well grab an hour's sleep.

"Tell me when you feel like talking about what happened yesterday," Trust answered.

"Sure. I'm still doing a little assimilating."

"Whenever you say. You got something to read?"

Blackford pulled the paperback from his pocket. "The girl is beginning to realize that the guy isn't so bad after all. The suspense is killing me." He went upstairs, lay down on his bed, and wondered whether the Central Intelligence Agency had anybody in the Soviet Union from whom it received regular information. His eyes scanned the pages of the novel, but did not transmit their meaning. He closed his eyes:

Dear Lloyds of London:

I am a Soviet scientist, working on the most closely guarded national enterprise. Now I have decided regularly to inform the Central Intelligence Agency on the progress of my unit in the Soviet Union. I would like a life insurance policy. I am forty years old and extremely strong, as witness that I spent eight years in a slave labor camp in the Arctic and survived. Would you please cite me your rates as I should like to take out a policy of one million pounds on my life, payable to my wife, Tamara. In the event she is not living at the time of my death, I should like the beneficiary of that policy to be Mr. Blackford Oakes, also known as Julian Booth, also known as just plain Harry. He is one of the nicest young men I have ever met, and I would like to make this gesture of appreciation. Write to me c/o Satellite Center, Tyura Tam, Russia. If there is anything I can do for Lloyds of London at T-T, please do not hesitate to advise

Your servant,
Viktor Kapitsa

Blackford reminded himself that it was unprofitable to go on this way, in this line of work. *"Et ne nos inducas in tentationem,"* he remembered from his Latin studies at Greyburn, the midterm exam at which required the translation of the Lord's Prayer into Latin. The French version, *"ne nous laissez pas* succomber *à la temptation,"* he thought, recalling his activities of the evening before last, was far less realistic.

If led to temptation, the chances were overwhelming he would succumb. And now he was leading poor Viktor straight into it. But "poor Viktor" wasn't what this whole enterprise was about. Insufficient attention to strategic objectives created Vorkuta in the first place, and Viktor, if apprehended now, would almost surely in one sense suffer less than he had suffered already—he would simply be executed. Isn't it justifiable to lead people into temptation, to expose them to danger—in order to prevent the recurrences, on a systematic scale, of such spectacles as he had witnessed at Dohany Street in Budapest last November? Wasn't Viktor better situated than almost anybody to recognize this? Blackford experienced that wave of frustration he had taken such pains to avoid. He forced himself to ask a simple question: Was he, or was he not, going to permit himself to get some sleep? When Trust woke him, it was seven o'clock.

Blackford washed his face, and joined the group downstairs. Viktor and Vadim were drinking vodka. Tamara and Anthony were sipping from wineglasses. Vadim switched to English, jabbered about the French political crisis, and quickly slid back into Russian. To Blackford's surprise, Tamara joined the English group rather than the Russian. She was amusing, inquisitive, altogether ingratiating. The dinner was a very special effort, to which Vadim had made numerous references in the course of the past two days. "You are entitled to one very great French cuisine," he said, "and the cook he has worked all day"—to prepare what proved to be the most extensive meal Blackford had ever eaten, and it gave him pleasure to see Viktor and—surprising, in the light of the experience at noon—Tamara go enthusiastically from the turbot, to the capellini, to the *sorbet au cassis,* the *poularde en feuilles,* the cheese, strawberries, and chocolate mousse. The three wines were, to say the least, appropriate, and Vadim insisted on bringing in the chef. Blackford whispered to Anthony that they really ought to bring in Congressman Rooney. When the chef appeared, Anthony began to sing "For He's a Jolly Good Fellow" in a French accent, and Viktor and Tamara caught the tune in time to join in the reprise. They went giddily into the living room for coffee, after which Blackford said he must be going and asked Vadim please to give him now whatever package it was he wanted delivered to Paris. Blackford said good night to the others, told them he would see them again in the morning and might even be able to bring in the first edition of *Le Monde.* Vadim excused himself.

In Blackford's room Vadim reported in a voice entirely sober: "Viktor he is cooperating. His terms are most pure and simple: (1) Tamara she is not to know nothing; (2) no chain of communications from us to him is to be formed—only the other way. He will not even listen to all the arrangements of Rufus, not even hear them. He has given to me, providing the understanding that I will not share it with *anyone,* the means he has elected for sending us 'my occasional communications.' He feels we must get him back to the delegation not later than tomorrow—the delegation it is returning to Russia on Sunday. We must rehearse in very good detail the cover story. He leaves that to us and 'your friend in Paris.'"

"Does he know who our boss is?"

"Interesting. Very interesting. He has not never brought up the subject. As far as Viktor is officially concerned, he has an arrangement—with me. Yes, he must most certainly know what I will do with the information. He could pass a truth test—and maybe they will give him one—that he has not knowingly been with American intelligence agents."

Blackford knew that polygraph tests didn't work that way, but said nothing. "Okay, I'm on my way. I'll see you whenever Rufus is through with me."

The drive went quickly, and without asking any questions the landlady gave him a key. Blackford opened the door and found himself face to face with an entirely naked stranger drying his buttocks with a large towel while talking uninterruptedly to a presence in the kitchen. He paused only to say, "Hi. You're Julian, I guess. So anyway, we got this real dumb sonofabitch and he says, 'I got the stuff one hundred percent purified.' Sonofabitch is an MIT bastard, you'd think he'd know his ass from an isosceles triangle, you can bet your ass he doesn't."

Rufus came out of the kitchen carrying a tray with a thermos of coffee. "Ah. Julian. This is Punston Hirsch, Julian Booth."

"Call me Punky." He had slipped on his shorts and T-shirt, and reached over and grabbed Blackford's hand with a grip, thought Blackford, that would have made John Wayne wince. "Howdy, Julian, howsa boy." He turned to Rufus. "Twelve fucking hours on that Herc, noisiest fucking plane ever built. I'd like to meet the designer. Know something, by the time I rode in one of those things a half hour, I coulda told the creep how to balance the engines better than they did, cut down the friction, increase the insulation: I'd like to send *that* designer to Russia to build *their* planes, we'd have a better chance to win the next war. Coffee? Shit, I didn't fly from Cape Canaveral to Paris nonstop to drink coffee, gimme some hootch. Here, kid"—he handed the rejected coffee cup to Blackford, who wasn't more than three or four years younger—"want some of this crap? It's hot, but I suppose you guys make other people taste things first." He laughed. "All *I* got to do is lift that mother up in the sky, that's all, while you people slow down the other team. This guy I was talkin' about, I'm not supposed to use names, anyway, so he says he's got the stuff purified. You begin by facin' the problem, it's got to go out as O_3. To do that, you got to convert two molecules of O_2 into one triple-atom molecule O_3 and that leaves the extra oxygen atom flyin' around like a horny tomcat lookin' for another loose oxygen atom to form O_2. The Russians—I pick this up from what you guys got from that feller—have got it licked. Got to figure out how to keep it pure all the way to containment and storage. Ya get trouble, I mean real trouble, I mean you blow up, boy, at any stage where there's impurities, hoses, couplings, valves, meters, seams, linings, lubricants, you name it. Ya get to see those pictures? Well I did, and man, those rockets, they're not going to go up without 170 tons of lift on the first stage rocket, I'm tellin' you. And they popped one of those babies the other day three thousand fuckin' miles, to Kamchatka." Blackford noticed with some amusement the pain on Rufus's face at the serial indiscretions of the scientist commonly acknowledged to be the leading Western authority on jet propulsion.

Rufus interrupted: "All we have here, Punky, is brandy. How about brandy and soda?"

"I'll take brandy without the fuckin' soda, thanks." He was sitting now on the couch, in shorts and T-shirt, his slacks and coat lying untended on the radiator. "Okay now, so I'll tell your boy Julian here exactly the questions to ask the Communist feller, it won't take all that long." He took a slug from the glass given him, and lit a cigarette.

"Before you begin, Punky, I've got a little business here with Julian. We'll go into the next room."

"Take your time. I'm feelin' a lot better after that shower and a little hootch, fucking Air Force doesn't give you any booze. Ride a Herc-30, they should give you morphine."

Rufus closed the door of the kitchen, and Blackford gave him the news of the decision of Viktor, and of his interlude with Tamara.

Rufus thought silently, leaning against the kitchen table. "I had the second message delivered to the embassy at one o'clock, giving them plenty of time to get an answer in tomorrow's *Le Monde*. I said"—he quoted from memory—"'Your terms are unreasonable. But we will meet you halfway. When the *Chekhov* is tied up at Bizerte, Kapitsa will reappear. Our contact in Bizerte will inform us within one hour that the vessel is docked. Do not attempt any treachery as you would greatly regret it. We agree that we are brothers. It is for you now to prove it. For the liberation army, Jean.'"

"What happens if the *Chekhov* ties up and nobody gets in touch with the captain?"

"Somebody *will* get in touch with the captain. An authentic Algerian insurrectionist. All he knows is that a collateral but unidentified Algerian cell in Paris contrived the delivery. No problem."

"So what am I to do?"

"Take down—you will need to take extensive notes on this one —what our friend Punky tells you. Get all the details you can from Kapitsa as early tomorrow as you can. The *Chekhov* could dock, if instructed to proceed at full speed, as early as noon. When we get the word from Tunisia, have Anthony drive the Kapitsas to Porte de Clignancourt. Let them out of the car to take a taxi to the hotel. They don't know where they were. The taxi that picked them up took them to a van and they were made to enter at gunpoint. They were blindfolded. It took them about two hours to get to their destination. During the period of their detention they were kept in a small farmhouse—there's a book in your bedroom at St.-Firmin illustrating typical farmhouses in France. Pick one out and get them to study the interior. They were not addressed by a single person while there. The cook who fed them was a male of swarthy complexion. There was someone else with a gun, also of dark complexion, with a moustache, guarding the only entrance to the farmhouse, day and night. At night they were locked into their bedroom. No telephones. Not a single word spoken, though they overheard the guard and the cook occasionally talking in a guttural French. Their line is very simple: They haven't the remotest idea who was using them for what purpose. I'm going to leave.

I've got a lot to do. I advise you to get back to St.-Firmin tonight, even if it's late. I'll call you in the morning."

He opened the kitchen door. "Well, Punky, our friend Julian here will take it all down, and do the best he can. I'll see you tomorrow. I understand you plan to fly back tomorrow night?"

"Yeah, and when they load ole Punky on that airplane, excuse the expression, they're gonna need four men, 'cause ole Punky is gonna be stiff as an ironing board, you bet, another twelve hours in that fuckin' tank." From his position, feet on the coffee table, he waved at Rufus and gave him a broad smile. "That's pretty good hootch, Rufus. Thank you, boy. You all come down to Cocoa Beach someday, and I'll look after you."

Rufus waved his thanks, said good-bye, and left, still impassive.

* * *

It was almost three in the morning. Punky's capacity for hootch was Rabelaisian, but it appeared to affect him not at all. His capacity to formulate and describe, Blackford noticed with awe, could not be improved on by any textbook writer. In turn Punky was impressed by the ready grasp of the questions by the young man whose background, to be sure, was clearly scientific. Finally, Blackford's notes complete, he gratefully accepted a proffered shot of the brandy, noting that this might be his last chance, the bottle being very nearly depleted. Punky was now reminiscing. "Wish I could take the credit for the breakthrough on the instrumentation, but if ever there was fuckin' serendipity, that was it. That feller from MIT—Van de Graaff—got the idea for the unit— he and John Trump—and he didn't have any reason to know that his unit's electron beam effect on the transistor crystals—that's what the Russian feller says is killin' 'em at Tyura Tam trying to shore up—is like fuckin' hormones. He teams up with a couple of electrical engineers and they form this company, see, High Voltage Engineering Corporation, Burlington, Mass., and begin cranking 'em out for commercial use. Goddamnedest concept. Do anything. Increase toughness of most plastics. Sterilize medical products that can't stand heat. Extend life of shelf foods. Know what Morganstern—Kennard H.—said about the E-beam? 'It's like discovering fire all over again.' Fuckin' A. An outfit in Westbury, Long Island, Morganstern's Radiation Dynamics, Inc., gets one of those units and Johanssen passes some transistor crystals through it, and *bang!* it's like Popeye takin' his stupid spinach. We got no troubles up at the top of our rocket, where the Commies got their troubles. Our problems are at the ass-end, the fuckin' fuel, which they got licked, and the leads this feller's given us are hot, and now we need just the answers to those questions you got down there, Julian, so be a real good boy and bring those back to me, and we'll give you a satellite for Christmas. Deal?"

"It's a deal, Punky." Blackford rose, and yawned, and tucked the notebook into his jacket pocket.

"So long, kid."

"So long, grandpa."

Punky smiled, and looking over his toes, in a position almost exactly horizontal, his head just slightly elevated on the back of the couch, he raised his drinking hand in salutation.

* * *

Blackford drove via the Porte Champerret, slipped fifty francs to the news vendor who was uncarting bales of newspapers, and took from him an issue of *Le Monde*. He reached Chantilly at daybreak, tapped out the code on the windowpane, and was admitted by the night sentry. He mumbled a good morning and headed for the kitchen, where he poured himself a glass of milk, and sat at the kitchen table, allowing himself a look at the headlines, which featured divers news of Algerian terrorism and French cabinet crises. Senator Humphrey had given a speech saying that arms control wouldn't work unless China was in on the deal, otherwise the Russians would use China as a loophole. He turned then to the classifieds and brought the lamp closer to see the fine print. He ran the table knife down the columns. It was there: "Dear Anna Krupskaya: Your terms are accepted. We shall expect the exchange before sunset." Well, thought Blackford, just what Rufus expected. So what else is new?

What else was new he saw only because of the inertial movement of his eyes. Three inches under the item marked for the attention of Anna Krupskaya was another: "Harry. I need to speak to you. Call LITtre 2535. Frieda."

He looked at his watch. Six-fifteen. Should he wait, consult Rufus? Impulsively he reached for the telephone and gave the number to the operator. A sleepy man's voice answered.

"Is Frieda there?"

"Who wants to talk to her?"

"Harry."

"What is Harry's last name?"

Blackford recognized the voice of Erno Toth.

"Harry Browne."

"When did Harry last see Frieda?"

"At the same time I last saw you, Erno."

"All right, Harry. She is very anxious to see you. Her—you have a pencil?"

"Yes."

"At home—she leaves for the office at eight-fifteen—she is at DUPont 1131. At the office it is TROcadero 3535."

"Thanks. Good luck, Erno."

"Good luck, Harry."

Chapter 22

ANTHONY WOKE BLACKFORD at nine, as instructed to do by the note appended to *Le Monde,* left outside Anthony's room.

"Long night, Black?"

"Yup," he yawned, accepting gratefully the coffee. "Did you remember to give Viktor and Tamara some peanut-butter sandwiches so they wouldn't go to bed hungry?"

"Not a bad performance, that dinner, you have to admit. I bet not all kidnappers feed their guests the way we do."

"That's right. Which reminds me, Anthony, Rufus gave strict orders that you're not to rape Tamara. Sorry about that. But you know, *salus publica, suprema lex?*"

"Look after your own *salus,* Oakes; Alouette isn't likely to."

"Anthony, shall we cut the crap?"

"After you, Blackford."

Blackford smiled. "Okay. What's going on?"

"Rufus called. He didn't know whether you had gotten the paper before leaving Paris. I told him your note was datelined 6:15 A.M. I've talked to Vadim, he's talked to Viktor, and there's no problem. He'll spend as long as you need with you, but assumes he can answer any questions he has the answers to in two or three hours. He doesn't, for some reason, carry blueprints with him."

"I was with a character last night. An expert. Maybe *the* expert. I know now exactly what our guys want, and how to ask for it. Here's a question: Do we want Tamara there? I'd think not, though she'd help with the English. I suppose Vadim can get through to us what Viktor has to say. Let's put it up to Vadim. Go talk to him while I get showered. Tell him for what it's worth, my vote is to keep her away. It makes it easier for him."

Outdoors the atmosphere was charged with electricity, snorts of thunder alternating with shafts of brilliant yellow light. The mood in the drawing room was one of high expectation. Blackford began by handing them the volume devoted to French farmhouses, and indicating the particular farmhouse whose features they should commit to memory. It had been decided that Tamara would devote herself to that assignment while, in the study, Blackford and the two Russians went at the scientific questions. Anthony would quiz Tamara and stand by the telephone. Suddenly Blackford remembered Frieda, excused himself, and dialed the Trocadero number from the upstairs telephone.

He identified himself and she was quickly satisfied it was he.

"I am glad to hear from you, Frieda. Are you all right?"

"Yes. But I should see you. I have important information."

"Frieda, I'd love to see you, but I'm out of town, calling from long distance. I don't know my schedule exactly, but I could probably make it tonight. Is that okay?"

"Yes. When will you know?"

Blackford thought. "I'll call you as early as I can. But I'll call you no matter what before four o'clock. Tell me this: Is anybody following you?"

"Not that I know of. I have been very careful."

"Okay, see you later."

It occurred to Blackford that the day was going to be long. Well, a good idea to get started with Viktor.

* * *

It was noon when the meeting broke up. Blackford had found it a remarkable experience. Notwithstanding the language barrier, the extraordinary fluency of Kapitsa's scientific mind made possible a kind of transliteral communication. He felt as if he had listened to a lecture by Isaac Newton. Vadim too grasped both the problems and the answers. Blackford went to a typewriter and in forty-five minutes came back with a text which Vadim translated into Russian to an acquiescent Kapitsa, who nodded almost continuously, reaffirming the accuracy of this transcript of his explanations. By one o'clock they were hungry, and fatigued by the concentrated session. At lunch Tamara exercised herself by describing the narrative of their detention, exhibiting to Viktor the illustrations of the rooms they had occupied. Anthony showed them a map of Paris and indicated the gate where the "van" would stop, its door opened, the Kapitsas released. "There are always taxis in the neighborhood. Your job is merely to take a taxi to the hotel. I would suggest you go to your hotel room and call Viksne from there. He will no doubt be full of instructions as well as questions. We have no way of knowing what he has told the members of the delegation. You can safely assume he hasn't told them the truth. Probably said you were sick. He may want to fancy you up with some scars—a lingering cough, or something."

Tamara said, though not without an evident sense of strain, "We'll handle Viksne. Remember: Viktor is very important to Viksne. He will be anxious to believe the whole business had only the Algerian angle."

Blackford and Tamara, the weather having settled to a balmy sunshine, strolled down to the lake, while Vadim and Viktor talked fervently, on the tacit assumption that they would never talk again.

Blackford hoped the conversation would be casual. But she came right to the point. "Julian, Viktor has not told me so, but I expect he has made an arrangement with you. I have been very compliant in this situation, and I honor Viktor's commitment. You put it to me very forcefully at the restaurant, and I have no answer to what you say: He *is* the man to define his own happiness, and establish his own priorities. But one day he may need help. I have no way of knowing whether you have people in Russia who might be in a position to help him. But I must have a contact point. With you or with Vadim. If I need to cry out for help, I must know in which direction to cry out."

Blackford made a snap decision.

"Do you have anyone on the outside now with whom you communicate?"

"I have never met her, but I exchange greetings and occasional photographs with Viktor's older sister. She married a Swedish diplomat during the war, and got out. Though she and Viktor haven't seen each other since 1941, they are very close and correspond frequently."

"Give me her name and address. I will arrange it so that she can get in touch with me wherever I am, within a few hours. You should know that it would be dangerous to attempt to get messages out through her, and therefore you shouldn't use the channel except in the case of emergencies."

"No. You give *me* an address in America. I will use it, through Sweden, if necessary. I hope *never* to use the channel." She paused, and looked up at him—they were sitting casually on the grass, watching, inattentively, the swans go listlessly by. "I didn't mean to make that sound unfriendly. In other circumstances, I would like to be your . . . friend." She paused and looked down. "Even *that* isn't well said. I *am* your friend. I admire what you are doing, and how you do it. I mean, in better circumstances I would hope to see you, and"—suddenly the self-assured astrophysicist seemed bashful—"Viktor I am sure would also like to be your friend."

Blackford leaned over and kissed her lightly on the forehead. He pulled out her pocket notebook and scribbled. "Here's the address and pseudonym of Vadim. I move about a lot, but he stays pretty well in . . . that address. He wouldn't give it out, for Viktor's sake. But I now have it. Vadim will know how to act. He is better situated than I am to deal with the higher authorities."

"I'll memorize it and won't forget it."

At three-fifteen the telephone rang. Trust spoke with Rufus, who then asked for Blackford. Handing the receiver over, Trust whispered: "It's all set."

"Good afternoon, Rufus. And how many pounds of chestnuts would you like delivered this evening?"

For a man who missed nothing, Rufus was also expert at ignoring such sallies. "Your morning's notes. I'll want them. Let us meet again at Mme. Rondpoint's at six."

"Okay. Rufus, is there any reason you know of why I can't make a dinner date?"

"Do you believe what you have to explain to our friend of last night will take you more than an hour or two?"

"No. I'm ready for him."

"Very well. In that case you should be free for dinner. Goodbye."

Blackford telephoned Frieda. "Shall we have dinner?"

"That would be especially nice."

"You say where. And remember, I'm still hot."

"You are what?" He explained. She gave him an address. "What time?"

"Eight o'clock."

Chapter 23

BLACKFORD ROSE and stretched his arms after ninety minutes of intensive interrogation by Punky, Rufus listening in, adding here and there a comment or two, the adroitness of which persuaded Blackford that somewhere, sometime (concerning Rufus's background no one was presumed to know anything, let alone encouraged to prod), Rufus had acquired the training that equipped him to follow esoteric scientific talk. Punky was all over Blackford, tearing apart his notes, talking himself through formulae explicit and adumbrated, asking questions which Blackford did, or did not, have the answers to, snorting approval, neighing disgust, expressing himself variously in obsequious wonder at, or in high Texan contempt for, Soviet science. On one aspect Punky was reduced to sheer awe: the Soviet mastery of the primary lift-mechanical aspect of the missile. "Tell ya, boy, those fuckers, they're gonna come 'roun' one of these days—I'm not talkin' about the year 2000, either—an' they gonna say: 'Boys, y'all wanna fight? Jus' give us, oh—Berlin for sure—Cairo; the sheeky-boys an' all that oil—jus' for starters. You want somethin'? *Waal,* mebbe if y'all behave, you get to keep Key West.' Yup, rate they're goin' that's what we'll be hearin', you bet you' ass, Rufus."

Rufus came as near to impatience as he ever did. "Come on,

Punky. They've got a launch-lead on us, and they fooled us about the direction they were headed. But if I understood you, you've now *got* the answer to what's been holding us back, and in six months or so you can go with it. You forget, they *don't* have an answer to the instrumentation problem: *We* do. We've got the scientists, we're developing the know-how, and if we weigh in on the technological war on a crash basis, they'll be worrying about holding on to the Ukraine in ten years, not about taking on Berlin."

"Atta boy, Rufus," said Blackford, standing now, and leaning against the book-lined wall of the study. "Rufus," Blackford addressed Punky in solemn accents, "is the illegitimate son of Knute Rockne. Now it isn't widely known that Knute Rockne had any illegitimate sons. M-G-M wouldn't permit it. But M-G-M just wasn't watching that night, and Rufus came into this world to cheer on the Big Team, for the Big Fight, eh Rufus?"

Rufus's smile was strained, but then it always was, and for the tenth time since knowing him, Blackford felt ashamed at teasing someone whose comprehensive skills mattered so greatly. It appeared now assured that the United States would launch the first satellite. And the contrivance of that was: the work of Rufus. He felt a child's obligation to retreat, though he knew it would be clumsy. "Punky, you're going back to Florida with a lot of information you didn't have. What's done with it is up to you and up to the people who control the purse strings. Lecture them, not Rufus. Fair enough?"

"Fair enough, kid, y'all did a real good job; now if you could figger a way ah could git my ass back to Florida without ridin' that Sherman tank . . ." his eyes went back to his notes. "Ah think it's time for a drink"—he looked at his watch. "7:35. Ah tol' 'em at the base ah'd be there 'roun' nine, they could warm up the fucker, maybe see if they could fit in an extra propeller, fucker travels 290 fuckin' miles per hour, might as well go back on a sailboat."

Rufus was prepared, and from the kitchen brought a bottle of scotch, ice, and soda. Punky grabbed the bottle nonchalantly, never taking his eyes off his notebook, and, with his pencil, began a free-sketch drawing. Blackford motioned to Rufus. In the kitchen Blackford said:

"I have an engagement for dinner tonight with Frieda. She's the girl I told you about who saved me at the necktie party the other day. I don't know what she has in mind, but figured you ought to know about it."

Rufus looked vaguely concerned. He paused, sat down on the kitchen chair. "Let's think out loud. This is Friday. On Wednesday you were supposed to be executed. The executioner, a double agent, disappears. He doesn't report back to his boss. His boss is almost certainly Bolgin himself, or Bolgin's Hungarian operative, who has been spending time in Paris. In any case, Bolgin must have known about the operation, and approved it. What does he do when he doesn't hear again from—was it Joseph Nady?"

"That's how it sounded."

"He wants to find out what happened, so he might well go after one of the two other members of the Hungarian execution squad. We don't know whether he knew who they were. Let's assume—always safer, Blackford—that he did. So he finds the girl, Frieda. He's looking for you. He lets her dig you up—oh yes, Blackford, I noticed the ad in *Le Monde*. It certainly isn't clear how he would turn her into a sitting ambush for you. So let's suppose the worst—always a good idea, Black. Oh. I said that already. Let's assume the worst: He gets hold of her, and comes up with some argument she swallows, about how you can be useful to her and other freedom fighters struggling to get out. A tall order, but Bolgin doesn't mind complicated problems. The point of it is: Don't meet her at her rendezvous. Unsafe."

Blackford's face expressed his exasperation.

"Listen, Rufus, this girl is tough, and she believes in me. She's not going to lead me to the slaughter."

"Correction. She's not going to lead you *willingly* to the slaughter. What restaurant did she propose?"

"Chez Anna near Palais de Chaillot. What do you propose?"

"Simple. Write a note"—he handed a piece of paper to him, leaned back, and began dictating as if to his secretary. "'Dear Frieda: For purposes of security I have reason to believe we should meet at another restaurant. The name and address of it are sealed in the enclosed envelope. Don't open it until you get into a taxi. I'll be waiting for you.' Inside the second envelope write down, 'Voltaire, 27 Quai Voltaire.' We'll have the envelope delivered to her at Chez Anna. If she opens the first envelope, takes it with her and leaves the second envelope unopened when she walks out of the restaurant—alone—and if she is not followed, then it is reasonable to assume she is neither actively colluding with someone nor being followed."

"Who will know?"

"I will," said Rufus. He yawned. "It occurs to me that right about now, I have absolutely nothing to do until tomorrow. Kapitsa is back with the Soviet delegation, Punky will be leaving here in five minutes, and I don't mind in the least taking a little exercise myself in the simple disciplines. Good practice. If she opens the second envelope—gives any sign at all of looking into the second envelope, or if she is followed out, or if her cab is followed, I'll call you at Voltaire's, and when she arrives, she will find you absent—and safe."

Blackford smiled. "Okay, Rufus. You really *do* think of everything." The admiration was genuine: Here was the great master intelligence strategist, willing to do a gumshoe's work. . . . Well, Blackford supposed, Rubinstein probably plays nursery tunes for his grandchildren. He went back to badinage. "Got any ideas what we ought to eat?"

"I have ideas about what you shouldn't eat, Blackford, but they are old-fashioned and unlikely to appeal to you."

In the living room, Punky's tie was on and his seersucker jacket. He carried his overnight bag, and Blackford guessed it would require a professional wrestler to loosen the grip he had on it and its sacred contents.

"So long, y'all. Don't forget, next time you're in Cocoa Beach, you look for Punston Hirsch. It's not in the phone book, but," he winked, "you can get it either by calling the White House or askin' any of the girls in town where Punky lives." He grinned boyishly, shook hands, and walked out. Rufus watched through the window until Punky's driver pulled away.

"You know something, Rufus? It probably takes somebody who finds 290 miles per hour caterpillar-slow to devise a satellite that will travel at 17,000 miles per hour."

Rufus signaled to Blackford. "Let's go. I'll drop you at Voltaire's and go on to Chez Anna."

* * *

It was just after 8:30 when Blackford spotted her. He sat in a table in the womb of a concave booth of which there were a half dozen in a row in the slightly shabby Empire-style main dining room. Blackford had been sipping a kir and reading the newspaper, beret and glasses in place, having given a name to the maître d'hôtel in the event of a telephone call. Frieda sat down quickly, before Blackford had time to rise and help her. She wore a simple blouse, starch-white, and a fine gold chain necklace, and around her wrist a knitted cotton bracelet, interweaving the colors of the Hungarian flag. She wore only a trace of lipstick, and her dark eyes were liquid.

Blackford began. "I'm sorry about the precautions. The problem is whether József's friends are following you."

"They are not," she snapped, "but they are anxious to."

Blackford signaled the waiter, and she asked for a dry vermouth, and *le menu*." Blackford said make that two. "Tell me about it?"

"That afternoon, after we came back, I went first to work—I had called in the morning and said I was sick. After the office closed I couldn't get József out of my mind, so I went to his apartment and told the landlady—she's Hungarian, and recognizes me—that József had called me from out of town, and asked me to collect some things. She let me in, and closed the door. The first thing I did was take the picture of Theo out of the frame." She opened her purse, and brought it out. Blackford winced at seeing a picture of a face he had last seen hanging from a rope and swinging in the cold Budapest wind of November.

"I decided to search the apartment. I found in the drawer of his desk a book, a book of addresses and telephone numbers. I have it here." She produced it from her purse. "I began leafing through it. I recognized the names of many people we both know. The book dates back to . . . last fall. Then I looked for the Paris numbers—there weren't so many of those. There were familiar names, mine, Erno's, many others. But then there was a number"—she opened the book and held it so that Blackford could see—"that seemed unusual. It's two numbers, very neat, but opposite no name, in the 'B' section. One is a foreign number. The other, a Paris number.

"Well, I have a friend. Her grandparents were Hungarian, and still live there, though Madeleine went to school in Paris, and works for the telephone company. I asked her to find out for me whose telephone it was, and yesterday morning she gave me the answer: It is the private telephone of the military attaché of the Soviet Embassy."

Blackford whistled. "On the other hand I guess that shouldn't surprise us." Frieda had begun to eat her soup, and Blackford ordered some white wine.

"No, not now after what we know now about József. But I conceived a plan, and I have reached the part where I didn't think I should go on with it without first consulting you."

Blackford looked at her in a different light. Theophilus had always spoken of her shyly, protectively. That day, at the barn near Fontainebleau, her role had at first been passive, leaving it to the men to do the wrangling. But having made up her mind, it was she who had been the decisive factor. Blackford sensed the alarming possibility of a crossed circuit. He had a score to settle with Bolgin, all right; but he had no desire to distract him from his present preoccupation with Algerian kidnappers.

"Consult me about what you *are going to do,* or about what you *have done?*" Blackford asked.

"About what I have done."

"Oh my God, Frieda," he said, without volunteering any elucidation.

"Oh my God what? I realize you were the specially selected victim of the operation the other day. But first they took *my* country, then they hanged *my* fiancé, then they tortured to death the woman who got *me* out of the country, and now they tried to use *me* as a member of an execution squad to assassinate an American who tried to help Theo. And who *did* help me." She looked up, and her eyes were full, as she extended her hand to Blackford, grasping it warmly, passionately.

"What have you done?"

"I called the number, and a voice answered. I said: 'I wish to speak to the military attaché.' The voice replied, 'About what?' I said, 'About József Nady.' He said, 'What about József Nady?' I said, 'Do you or do you not wish to have information about him?' There was a silence, and I could hear that the telephone was being switched off. Then the voice came back, and it was much more pleasant. The man said, 'Are you where I can call you back?' I said, 'No'—and offered no alternative arrangements. I am aware that there are techniques for tracing telephone calls—I was using a public phone, away from my apartment and office. So I said, 'If you wish to know where you can find József Nady and the American, you will have to follow the instructions I will give you on this telephone.' He said: 'When will you call?' I said, 'I will call you tomorrow at 10 A.M.'"

"What," asked Blackford with increasing awe, "do you propose to say tomorrow at 10 A.M. to Colonel Bolgin?"

"Is that his name?"

"Yes," he said. "Boris Bolgin. He is the top KGB official in Europe. I've actually met him. He's good with the soft exterior, but he's been trained to do the kind of thing that Stalin approved of. The business last Wednesday shows a certain imagination: stringing *me* up for *betraying* Theo—and using Theo's fiancée as part of the execution squad. Not bad. What do you have in mind to say to him?"

"I don't know," she said simply. She dropped her fork on her plate, looked up at him, and smiled with manifest pleasure at her decision: "I shall say to him whatever you like! At one end of the table," she said matter-of-factly, "we could arrange to kill him. At the very least, we could . . . well, get you your money back. But it occurred to me that perhaps there was something *you* might specially want from Bolgin."

Right, Blackford thought. He would like Bolgin's balls, just, well . . . for instance.

Frieda sipped her coffee and downed her liqueur. "I think it would be useful—and amusing—to think about it, and I suggest we do that"—she looked at him now directly in the eye—"at my apartment." Blackford's pause was only barely noticeable. "I think," he said, summoning the waiter, "that we would have privacy there," and he returned her gaze directly, "to do whatever we want."

"I am prepared," she replied quietly, "to do whatever you want."

"I think," he said, feeling that telltale tightness in his throat, but smiling, "that we should agree to act jointly."

"In that case," she said getting up, "we had better begin."

* * *

He came upon a terrible hunger. He had difficulty, in the climax, in holding her firm the more so through his own wild excitement as, in the dim light that perforated her underthings, strewn in her haste over the little bed lamp, he peered into her eyes. She was looking at him now with exhibitionistic passion as her pale, full breasts broke out in splotches of mottled light brown while her thighs gripped him and with her hands she stroked him, with a desperate milking action. Throughout, he gave himself totally, and once, in his writhing imagination, felt himself caught tightly, finally, in her noose, which drew him together suffocating, exhilarating, released only just in time for air; and then renewing its threat, its black, exacting embrace. It was midnight before, tenderly, he relaxed his hands, and bent over her face, to kiss her gently above the always-open eyes, and whisper to her, inquisitively, unchidingly, "Was that me, or Theo?"

"It was you. It was you, acting for myself. And acting also for Theo."

It had become possible for her to mention Theo other than in tones that required an empathic shudder of deferential solemnity; and Blackford too—for the first time—could think of the young Theo, with the wistful, trusting, beardless, dark-skinned boy face, talking, smiling, with a mug of beer in front of him, blotting out the convulsive, tortured death mask that had planted itself permanently in Blackford's inventory of nightmares.

She went on. "I should have known. I *would* have known. We were all three of us together, what, three, maybe four times? After ten minutes with you, I should have known it wasn't you who betrayed him. Revolutions—counterrevolutions—counter-counter-revolutions—they take away your judgment. We *know* Theo was not good at seeing through people. How can I say I was any better at it? Both of us believed in József. So did Erno, and the others. But my belief in József was . . . different." She lay back on the pillow, talking up at the ceiling. Impatiently she kicked the bed sheet aside, and now their bodies were entirely illuminated by the soft, eccentric light from the bed stand. She continued speaking as he, with his left arm under her neck, used his right hand to stroke her breasts gently. "It was Theo's purity that made everyone associated with him, by that association, pure. Do you know that— Erno told me this—in Theo's presence, in the locker room, there were certain stories they just wouldn't . . . tell? I mean, stories— you must know—about what so and so did with this girl or that girl the night before? The kind of story Theo wouldn't ever talk about. . . . The kind *you* wouldn't ever talk about; I expect"—she did not move her head—"that you are . . . a little that way yourself, Harry." He found it a strain to be called Harry, a surrealist reminder of realistic vicissitudes—Blackford, shifting the frame of his thought, had a hard time believing the ribald story existed that hadn't been told in his presence. "Theo was not—as beautiful as you"—she turned, coquettishly, and ran her hand over his profile, slowly, from the top of his head to near his toes—"but he was beautiful all over. He was the best thing in Hungary, and one day there will be a monument in the public square. Do you think so, Harry?"

"I think there ought to be," said Blackford, though that part of him that was the engineer paused to wonder whether there were enough public squares to commemorate the martyrs of that revolution. Or would the job need to be done collectively? What an awful concession to the Communists. But then they did use up their victims at a rate that made individual commemoration so very difficult. What does one do, when one hears of *15 million prisoners* in a slave camp? Perhaps someone, someday, in a great book, would give life to those anonymous victims of ideology and evil. He declined to cop a plea by adding the qualifier, "and insanity."

Frieda rose, walked with aplomb out of the room, and returned in a few minutes wearing a beige nightgown and carrying a tray. She apologized for her quarters—the bedroom served also as the living room. "Don't bother with the bed; come, sit here." She pointed to the armchair alongside her own, with the coffee table between, on which she had set down the wine and glasses. Blackford located his shorts and began to put them on.

"Don't dress. Come as you are. Isn't that what you say?" He smiled, walked over, and sat down. She said it first.

"What are we going to do about Bolgin?"

Blackford, accepting the glass and raising it silently to her, said, "We haven't had time to give it much thought."

Now Frieda smiled impishly; and sipped the wine lasciviously. "Oh!"

"What's the matter!"

"I just thought of something!"

"What is it?"—instinctively, Blackford had risen.

"I have some caviar! I've had it since my birthday!"

"Your birthday has got to be today, right?"

"Of course!"

It had been a gift from the wealthy godparents of her friend at the telephone company, Hungarian expatriates, and she had thought it too shamefully expensive to consume.

"Harry, you know, the money?"

"Let's change the subject."

"I spent half of it. When I needed it desperately. The other half I don't need. I cashed it this afternoon." She opened the desk drawer and took out an envelope.

Blackford hesitated, and then took it, tossing the envelope in the general direction of his discarded jacket. "All this and caviar!" She opened the jar and brought out butter and French bread. "Listen to me, Frieda," he said as he applied the caviar with the faded table knife. "Colonel Bolgin, as I've told you, is the chief KGB operative in Western Europe. His decision to use, to my terminal disadvantage, the momentum generated by the execution of Theo wasn't aimed merely at *one* CIA operative who had been working Budapest. He happens to have some old scores to settle with me, and I guess it's safe to say that his hostility reflects the . . . well, consolidated hostility of his service. They have been tracking me—that we know. Otherwise they wouldn't have known to inform József that I was staying at the France et Choiseul. They had a dragnet out for me, still do. Now I simply don't know *why,* other than what I've told you—the settling of old scores. But from all of this we can deduce several possibilities. One of them is that by now Bolgin knows either that József is dead, or that he is detained—or that he has defected. József was probably capable of becoming a double agent, of double-crossing the KGB; but not—I'd guess—in your presence, or Erno's. He would never have acknowledged to you that—hah hah hah—he was actually the guy who hanged Theo. If instead of killing him I had merely overpowered him, and then driven him away in a car . . . who knows whether money would have brought him around? We'll never know.

"Now let's assume Bolgin deduces the obvious—that something went wrong in Operation Hang Harry. He's still going to want to know whether József is alive or dead. He's going to want to know how much if anything he has . . . spilled."

"There is a third possibility," Frieda interrupted.

"What?"

"That somehow you overpowered József from the beginning, in the car."

"In which case—how did *you* happen to dial Bolgin's number directly? How, unless you were suspicious, would you have known to say into the telephone what you did—that if the military attaché was interested in knowing the whereabouts of József Nady, you were in a position to give out that information?"

"All right. I agree. He figures I know what happened. That could mean I know where you are—or that I don't. You might be dead."

"Correct. So—stay with me. Bolgin will attempt, over the telephone, to arrange a rendezvous. He would *certainly* dispatch to that interview a subordinate. The head of KGB-Europe isn't going to walk into something he hasn't cased out, something blind. You can also assume that whoever he sends to that meeting will be followed by one or more agents. So from that moment on, they would know (a) exactly who you are; (b) where you live. From that moment on—*whatever* happened during the interview—you'd be a sitting target on their list."

"I assume I already am. I attend all the anti-Communist rallies, all the Free Hungary Committee meetings."

"So does much of Paris. Anyway, we know there's one concrete disadvantage in your meeting him: You're put on his active list. On the other hand, you don't really *have* to meet him—or his representative. You might be able to accomplish anything you set out to accomplish over the telephone."

"Like what?"

"Well, just thinking big for a minute, you could tell him József has been identified as a Soviet agent, and that he will be released only when Bolgin has arranged for the release of—you name it—some freedom fighter they haven't got around to executing yet."

"There are many of them still in prison, and we know their names."

"Well, that's one possibility, though the old coot would almost certainly ask for proof that József is still alive, and that isn't the easiest thing in the world to come up with." Blackford got up, and, oblivious of his nakedness, paced the cramped quarters. "I dunno. I haven't got a real hunch on this one. But I feel that keeping the contact live is useful. Frieda, there's a guy in town—a very important guy—in a way I work for him. I should talk to him. My guess is at this point you're better off just stringing Bolgin along. Calling in at ten tomorrow and saying something like, 'I know where József is and the American. What is it worth to you to know?' Their technique in these situations, by the way, is invariable: They try to set up a meeting. You should say flat out, 'No.' You'll also find that the KGB is incredibly stingy. They're used to lubricating their informers on vats of ideology and sprinklings of cash. So you might mention an extremely high figure—extremely high by their standards and see what the reaction is. Break it down. Tell them: 'Ten thousand dollars'—I don't have a slide rule, so it'll take me a while to translate that into francs—'for József, fifty thousand dollars for the American.' See what their reaction is.

It's important for several reasons to know how badly they want *me*. And, of course, it would be interesting to know how badly they want József."

"What do I say if they ask for proof that I know where József is?"

"Tell them you'll deliver his driving license."

"What if they want proof that I know where you are?"

"Tell them you'll send a picture of me reading this morning's edition of *Le Monde*."

"What will they say then?"

"That's what I think is worth finding out. But don't do anything till you hear from me."

Later, when the dawn came in and woke them, she whispered to him, "Will I see you again, Harry?"

"If I'm alive."

"Don't say that." Her tone was almost hysterically stern.

"Sorry. I mean, 'Yes.'" His fingers became, once again, active, and her body feints encouraged him, revived him, and the old sensation in the throat began to come back. Hands busy, he whispered to her hoarsely, "Frieda?"

"Yes, Harry."

"You should impose one more condition."

"What's . . . that?"

"Tell Bolgin he must stand up at the Comédie Française, halfway through the second act of *Boris Godunov*, and denounce Khrushchev."

"All right, *chéri*, I promise."

"Now, pay attention."

* * *

"And what," she asked dreamily an hour and a half later, "would he do for an encore?"

"Sometimes," Blackford said, eyes closed, "an encore becomes too much to ask."

Chapter 24

THE DELEGATION, tired by the long flight with the exasperating layover in East Berlin, tired also by the hectic academic and social activity of the week, was granted leave to spend the night in Moscow instead of merely pausing to refuel and proceeding on to Tyura Tam, as scheduled. "You all have rooms reserved in your name at the Metropole Hotel," Viksne had said paternalistically over the plane's loudspeaker as, nearing seven o'clock, they approached the airport. "Each of you will pick up an envelope, with the reservation slip, and a little bit of Welcome Home cash from the GIRD. Go out on the town, go to the ballet, have a good solid Russian meal, sleep late. The bus will pick you up at noon exactly at the hotel and we'll take the last leg of the flight back to headquarters." There were audible grunts of satisfaction from the half-dozen scientists who would now have an evening in Moscow before returning to the six-hundred-mile-square scientific enclave where they were hectically engaged in establishing Soviet dominance over space.

Viktor and Tamara checked into their room and quickly washed so as to begin their evening as soon as possible. They discussed alternatives. They could go to the ballet, but there would be a long line for the few unsold tickets. They could perhaps ring up a friend or two—but this had the disadvantage that under security regulations they would need to spend most of the evening in dissimulation about their present activity. They could attend a play—there were several—and also a poetry reading by Yevtushenko. Somehow these events did not fit their mood. And so they decided simply to walk. "We might try," Viktor said excitedly, "to retrace the route we walked on the night that I asked you to marry me." That greatly appealed to Tamara. "Of course, we won't wear the same clothes! Do you remember how cold it was that night?" "No," Viktor said, "I remember how warm I was that night."

Smiling, she adjusted around his collar the new tie she had bought him in Paris on their slim hard-currency allowance; and she dabbed herself behind the ears with the perfume he had bought her. They set out together into a perfect summer night. As they had done on the other occasion, they had no formal meal. A vodka here. A Zakuska there. A beer at Café S'ev'er'. Coffee and brandy at the Hotel National. It was well after midnight before they returned to the hotel, happy in the knowledge that they could sleep in as late as they wished in the morning.

At noon, as they lined up to enter the bus, Pyotr Viksne approached. "I say, Viktor Andreyevich. Apparently you and Tamara will not be returning on the same flight to Tyura Tam. They wish to speak to you"—he pointed in the general direction of the Lubyanka. "I suppose," he said with steel in his voice, "it is just one more formality involving the Algerian business."

Viktor knew. Knew instantly. Those eight years had given him entirely reliable intuitions in such matters. He looked quickly at Tamara. She was concerned, but there was none of that critical anxiety on her face that suggested she too knew. Viktor's mind raced. He cared now only that she be spared. In fact he had not told her about any arrangements he had made, had not even told her the nature of his conversations with Vadim and the Americans. Could he maneuver so as to spare her? For this and for this only he must struggle. His own disposition, as upon reaching Vorkuta, was simply to give up, to accept his fate. Back then, Vadim had saved him. Now he must save Tamara. How? He felt his stomach contract when the car drove up and a cropped-haired driver with the telltale shapeless double-breasted suit got out and opened the door.

"Are we going alone?" Tamara asked Viksne.

"Yes, I must accompany the delegation. But you are expected; do not concern yourself." He waved good-bye, while, with the same motion, he directed the KGB driver to proceed.

In the car they did not talk. They might have done so in German, or English, but dared not risk it. He turned to her as they drove down that stygian ramp into the huge building that sheltered the aorta of Soviet terror, and whispered to her: "Do not contradict me. Do not say anything. Understand?" He gripped her hand.

Standing at the landing area of the underground ramp between the two seated armed guards was a youngish man, balding, blond, corpulent, in civilian garb.

"I am Captain Uglich."

Viktor acknowledged the unsmiling bow, and recalled that there was a labor camp of the same name.

"Kindly follow me."

This required stamina. The elevator was not working, and it was a full ten minutes of stairways and corridors before Viktor found himself in a room of modest dimensions, with a screen at the far end, on which no image projected.

"Sit down, Professor," Captain Uglich said, and left the room. Viktor and Tamara sat down on two of the several hard-backed chairs in the dimly lit room. Sudenly they heard a voice coming in through an amplifier in the corner. It was the voice of Viksne.

"*So that, just to repeat, Viktor Andreyevich, from the moment you and Tamara were picked up by the taxicab driver, you exchanged not a word with your captors?*"

He heard his own voice replying. "*Not a word. Well, hardly. At first we had to ask such routine questions as where were the toilet facilities.*"

"*And you overheard no conversations during that period?*"

"*That's correct. The French exchanged between the fellow who took us in, the bodyguard, and the cook, we could not make out.*"

"*Was it a deep, guttural French?*"

"*My French is not that good, but such was my impression, and my wife's.*"

"*The man in the taxicab who drove you off, did you attempt to speak to him at all?*"

"*Yes, at first, especially when it became clear we were being abducted. But he wouldn't answer. As I say, we only heard him talk on a few occasions and always in rapid French to his fellow conspirators.*"

At that moment a picture flashed on the screen. It was a huge enlargement of Viktor and Tamara Kapitsa being addressed by a young man wearing a beret, sitting in the driver's seat of a French taxicab.

At the bottom of the screen the words slid across, as in a ticker tape: "OAKES, BLACKFORD. DEEP-COVER AGENT OF CIA. BORN AKRON OHIO, DECEMBER 7, 1925. EDUCATED SCARSDALE NEW YORK HIGH SCHOOL, GREYBURN ACADEMY ENGLAND, YALE UNIVERSITY CLASS OF 1951. FOUGHT AS FIGHTER PILOT 37TH AIR FORCE SQUADRON FRANCE 1944–45. RECRUITED SUMMER 1951. EXPERT IN GERMAN, WORKING KNOWLEDGE FRENCH. KNOWN TO HAVE BEEN ACTIVE IN OPERATION DOCKET #472-A GREAT BRITAIN 1951, OPERATION DOCKET #4977-C GERMANY 1952. SPOTTED PARIS AT HOTEL FRANCE ET CHOISEUL ON JULY 2, 1957."

The door opened to the august presence of the director himself. General Gleb Mamulov, ramrod-stiff, dressed in simple but perfectly tailored gray gabardine with an undefined military cut, and a tieless Stalin collar. Viktor and Tamara rose.

"You are under arrest, Professors Viktor and Tamara Kapitsa. Charged with high treason, under Article 58-1a and 1b, as agents of the international bourgeoisie under Article 58-4; spies (58-6); subversives (58-7); noninformers (58-12); and abettors of the enemy (58-3). Do you have anything to say?"

"Yes," Kapitsa said. "My wife is entirely innocent."

Mamulov gave a snort which alone must substantially have contributed to his ascendancy in the KGB. It was the quintessence of disbelief, contempt, impatience, and outrage. "She was in the room when you answered the questions of Viksne. She did not contradict your lies."

"I told her my life was threatened if she did so. The fact remains she was privy to no conversations between me and the Americans."

Mamulov did not answer. He nodded to Uglich. "Take them away."

* * *

Thirty-six hours later, at dawn, three cars drove out of the bowels of the Lubyanka and threaded their way to the Yaroslavski station. There the Trans-Siberian train lay preparing its 8 A.M. departure. One car, at the end, was completely closed off, the windows barred and sealed. At one end of the car was a substantial clinic in which two military doctors sat, smoking, at opposite ends of a card table.

"It's all very well to expect us to revive these fellows. But I'd rather take on Lazarus than this one coming up." He reviewed the medical report he had been given at midnight, when summoned. "It's easy to say 'Revival matter of state security.' They should have said that to the people who"—his eyes traveled down the page—"broke his jaw . . . blinded him in one eye . . . perforated his pancreas . . . broke six ribs. Hmm," he took a deep drag from his cigarette, "the other damage appears to be minor. Perhaps the personnel at the Lubyanka are engaging in a slowdown for higher wages."

"What about the girl?"

"Haven't touched her, just heavy sedation. She's been out for almost two days. But they want her too, up the line. We're to see that she stays weak, but revivable."

"How long have we got?"

"As usual, they don't give the destination. We're to do 'everything we can' in thirty hours. Did you check the supplies?"

"Yeah." The young doctor looked about him. "We got enough stuff here to treat a graduate of the Lubyanka Summa Cum Laude."

They went back to their smoking, and the younger man yawned. "Never did a pierced retina before."

"You'll learn," said his colleague consolingly.

Chapter 25

BLACKFORD MET with Rufus for breakfast, and told him about Frieda and Bolgin, and the impending rendezvous on the telephone. Rufus listened, got up, and, from between two books in the library, pulled a large manila envelope.

* * *

Twenty minutes later, from a public telephone booth, Blackford spoke with Frieda.

At ten exactly, again from a public telephone, Frieda rang the number of Colonel Bolgin, who picked up the telephone himself, having arranged to record the conversation on magnetic tape.

"You are the same gentleman as yesterday?" she spoke in French.

"Yes. They call me Valerian."

"They call me Olga."

"I am very anxious to see you, Olga."

"I am a friend of József, and he has told me to follow his instructions."

"Where is József?"

"His instructions include not to tell you or anyone else where he is. Something has happened that has made some of his friends suspicious. He is going to America, but he is willing to do work over there for your friends if he is convinced he is safe. Meanwhile, I have a negative and a print for you."

Bolgin's heart began to pump excitedly. It had worked! *The very day after the kidnapping of Kapitsa, the kidnapper had been punished!* Moscow would like that. And there would be no end to the ramifications. It could even be suggested—why not?—that KGB justice was involved and was summary—if Moscow decided to go public, i.e., within the international intelligence fraternity, in the matter of the CIA's kidnapping of Kapitsa.

To be sure, it would have been useful at this point to get hold of Oakes alive, and question him. But they had retrieved Kapitsa as of yesterday afternoon, after all; and in due course, Bolgin meditated with satisfaction, Kapitsa would be most . . . thoroughly . . . questioned about his cock-and-bull Algerian story. Meanwhile: the picture!

His bargaining instinct asserted itself. He would feign only moderate interest in it. "Oh yes, the picture. Is it your plan to mail it to me?"

"Please, Valerian: I am busy. And I am about to cut off this conversation. I will call you from another telephone at exactly ten-thirty. The price is ten million francs. But József wants it in dollars. Twenty thousand dollars." Frieda hung up.

* * *

At ten-thirty, when the telephone rang, Bolgin picked it up. "Ten thousand dollars, and that is the top price."

"József instructed me not to bargain. The picture can, alternatively, be turned over to the Sûreté Nationale with an explanation as to how it happened, where the body is buried, and who gave the instructions."

Bolgin had a reliable instinct on the matter of when bargaining would work, and when it wouldn't. *"Eh bien. D'accord. Vingt milles."*

Before he could begin to stipulate arrangements, Frieda proceeded: "József says you are to send a woman from your department to the ladies' room on the second floor of the Galeries Lafayette. She is to arrive at exactly noon: in ninety minutes, approximately. There are six stalls. I'll be occupying the end toilet. The toilet next to it will have a sign on it—OUT OF ORDER—I'll tip the attendant to put it on, to make certain it will be unoccupied. Your woman is to open that stall. I will slide the envelope under the partition as soon as she has slid the package of bills under the partition. She can examine the photograph. When she raps on the partition, I will pick up the package and count the bills. *She is to stay in the toilet stall fifteen minutes.* Do you need me to repeat this? Oh. One more thing. József says you may include in the package the name of any contact in Washington or in New York if you wish József to have further dealings with you."

"I have the details," Bolgin snapped, and put down the telephone.

* * *

At ten minutes to one, Sverdlov's secretary, two years out of a KGB academy, returned perspiring from her mission in the large downtown department store. She handed the envelope to Sverdlov, who, as instructed, took it directly up one flight of stairs to the office of the military attaché, dropping it on Bolgin's desk. Bolgin's fingers shook as he reached for it. He opened it and slid out the 8 by 10 print. The background was appropriately grisly. The helter-skelter wine casks on the floor, the fixed end of the rope disappearing at an angle into the dark void, beyond the reach of the flashbulb. The dull blue shirt and inert, long slim legs; the arms bound behind; the face, cocked over by the noose, disfigured. Bolgin, his heart once again pounding, reached for his magnifying glass.

He stared at the face of the dead man. The blondish hair, loosely cut. The regular features, the swollen cheek. He felt a jet of ice run up his spine. He sat motionless, his mind racing. Sverdlov wondered that so professional a man as Colonel Bolgin should be taking such voluptuary satisfaction, even in such a work of counterintelligent art. Sverdlov was fascinated by the fixity of Bolgin's attention to the photograph.

Finally Bolgin slid the print back into the envelope and looked up. His voice was preternaturally steady.

"Well done. I shall meditate the uses to which we shall put the photograph—after consulting with Moscow."

Sverdlov, though disappointed that he had not been offered a view of the expensive photo, snapped his heels together and left. Bolgin, alone, dug his nails into the sides of his face—until he felt moisture at his right index finger. Alarmed, he walked over to the mirror. He had actually drawn blood on his right cheek. Calmly he went into the bathroom's medicine closet and applied the styptic pencil. As he looked into the mirror he said to himself, out loud, in exaggeratedly emphasized English, "Only you, Rufus, would think of it. Sell me, for ten million francs, a picture of József Nady on the perfect, the beautiful gallows prepared for Blackford Oakes. You knowing—goddam you, Rufus—that probably only *I*, Boris Bolgin, could tell the difference."

Chapter 26

"I'LL HAVE," the moustache seemed to aim its skepticism directly at the menu, "—is the pompano really fresh?"

"Yes, Mr. Secretary." They still called him that. At least, the waiters did. Mostly, he reflected, they called him other names, though it had been a while since anybody had referred to him as "The Red Dean." He had been secretly amused when that had happened. Senator McCarthy at his press conference had professed to be confused over whether the questioner had been referring to the Secretary of State or to the notorious fellow-traveling Dean of Canterbury Cathedral, who during the period was touring centers of native culture lecturing on the private virtues and public accomplishments of Joseph Stalin. McCarthy! Dead three months now. That death had given the former Secretary the opportunity, progressively rare, to knock off a Latin motto. "How do you spell 'mortuis,' Mr. Secretary?" one reporter—obviously not from the New York *Times*—had asked. *"De m-o-r-t-u-i-s nil nisi bonum,"* he had repeated, reflecting that to translate the phrase would appear patronizing, though as a matter of fact he was through caring whether the press thought him patronizing. It did occur to him, with that instinct which, after all, had kept him in public life for so many years, that he should arrange to see to it that word got out to Independence as to the meaning of it, so that when the old man called, which he was sure to do on getting the news, they could chuckle together. "I thought it a diplomatic way out, Mr. President," he could hear himself saying, and that would sound mellifluous, counterpointing what he was certain to hear over the telephone from the former President about the late senator. Great heavens—he arrested his musing.

"Fresh, you say, very well. Bring me some chilled Chablis—*Villages*, 1953—with it, and also iced tea."

"I'll have the same." It was a strange habit for a man as decisive as the Director. He *always* ordered the same as his guest. Indeed, so ingrained was the habit that when he had more than one guest, he would order the same as the guest who had given the immediately preceding order. The former Secretary was forever pledging to himself one day to order something revoltingly exotic —say, fried rattlesnake—and see whether the Director would say, "I'll have the same." The trouble was, they never ate together at restaurants that made much of fried rattlesnake.

"It's been a busy week, Dean."

"Indeed. May I assume that the Soviet claims for its ICBM tests are exaggerated?"

"You may do nothing of the sort. They are correct."

"So that the skepticism expressed yesterday morning by the Department of Defense was—calculated?"

"Yes. The Soviets are not yet aware that our little sky-bug is working on all engines and monitoring their—quite dismaying, by the way—successes. A little skepticism throws them off the track."

"Ah yes, but the results of your Paris venture are surely bearing fruit?"

"Indeed they are. At Houston, at Huntsville, and at Canaveral, the information turned them right around, and there is confidence we will work out the launch problem within months."

"That is very good news. Have I congratulated you?"

"No. But it was a very clean operation. Rufus deserves great credit."

"Ah Rufus, the indispensable Rufus. Yes. Tell me—if you care to—are we left with an active informant at Tyura Tam?"

"As far as we know. We haven't got in anything from him, but that doesn't especially surprise me. He warned our representative that his communications would be fitful. Besides, it will presumably be a while before he accumulates enough confidential information to warrant a message. We cleaned him out."

"Splendid. The President used some rather—straightforward—language this morning in rebuking our friends the Soviets for declining to go forward with the disarmament proposals."

"If you think that was straightforward, you should have heard the language he used in the Oval Office."

"I must confess to you, Allen, it distresses me to hear as I do from time to time that the President actually *is* surprised by such maneuvers, by such . . . tergiversations."

"It isn't so much that he's surprised, Ike just gets sore when he sees the sanctimony in which the refusals are invariably packaged."

"Yes, well I see his point; that is unquestionably one of the most irritating aspects of public life, Communist rhetoric."

"Did you see where Hsinhua in Peking accused him of 'insufferable arrogance' for agreeing to permit U.S. newspapermen to tour China?"

"Yes. I confess to having been rather disappointed. I had thought that phrase reserved to describe me. I have not seen it used since I left office."

"But Dean, you don't understand, it *was* true about you, but it's not true about Ike."

"I question whether this pompano is fresh."

The Director was pleased with his checkmate. "Your reply, Dean, was a classic example of *ignoratio elenchi,* as Joe McCarthy would have reminded you."

"Joe McCarthy is, at this moment, otherwise preoccupied, I should imagine. I wonder, do you suppose in Purgatory they are making him sign on as a member of the American-Soviet Friendship Committee?"

"Dean, on the matter of your trip."

"Yes?"

"I think under the circumstances you can be even more optimistic than you had planned on the matter of our being *first* up with the satellite. A little optimism is in order, particularly now that the Soviets have decided to be exhibitionistic with their ICBM technology. The French are in a fearful tizzy, and for one whole fifteen-minute period their ambassador left the subject of Algeria alone in talking to Foster, and asked him to level on the rocket business."

"What did your brother say?"

"What you'd expect. And lengthily: We're getting there . . . we're having trouble with a tightwad Congress and myopic Democrats, but we have every confidence . . . etc., etc., etc."

"That sounds like your brother."

"This Chablis is very good."

"That's why I ordered it."

"Another thing. You'll be seeing Macmillan, of course?"

"Of course."

"Tip him off. You saw yesterday he told Commons he was going to ask us to pool our H-bomb information with him? He's scheduled over here the last week in October, so you'll be seeing him ahead of time. Tell him *not* to bring up the subject with Ike. Ike's convinced the Brits haven't ferreted the Communist agents out of there, and I personally think he's correct. Anyway, Ike has said no, and it would be easier not to have to say no directly to Macmillan."

"Yes, I see what you mean. Summit conferences that avoid sundering questions are always to be preferred."

"I wish you had used a few sundering questions at Potsdam."

"Ah, we did. And Stalin gave in on just about every point."

"Good old Joe."

"If you desire to tease me about a famous mislocution by a great Democratic President, you should do so at a time when I am relieved of such inhibitions as I labor under as your guest."

"Jesus, Acheson, I bet you were insufferable even as a schoolboy."

"My first name is Dean, not Jesus; and the answer to your question is: I was."

They walked out together, the Director with his pipe belching out smoke, the former Secretary affecting to be asphyxiated by the fumes.

Chapter 27

IT HAD BEEN a pleasant late afternoon, except for the airplanes. Blackford and Sally had listened to the outdoor concert on the Potomac. The Opera Society of Washington had given a recitalist-performance of *Madame Butterfly,* but the late summer wind direction brought air traffic on final approach directly over the five thousand people sprawled on the grass and sitting on the benches on the west bank of the Potomac and at one point it sounded as though Lieutenant Pinkerton had compounded his perfidy by bringing in the entire United States Air Force to retaliate for Pearl Harbor. But here and there the music broke through, and it was lovely, and so was Sally, in a white and beige summer dress, with the little pearls in her ears that peeked out through her sunny brown hair. They had not once mentioned Subject X, Blackford's profession as impediment to their marriage; moreover, she was greatly excited at having been invited that morning by the *Sewanee Review* to review two books on the eighteenth-century British novel.

"Will you read my review, after I've written it?"

"Of course."

"I appreciate that. Especially since I don't read your obituaries after you kill people."

"That really is a pity. I think I may have developed a new art form. And you may be the last to discover it. Wouldn't that embarrass you professionally?"

She couldn't answer, because she had just bitten off a large hunk of hot dog. He took the advantage: "Do you have time to do any extracurricular reading?"

"Of course. What now?"

"Have you read *Parkinson's Law?*"

"No, should I?"

"Yes. Everyone should. It may be the only thing that will finally destroy the Soviet Union—the weight of its own bureaucracy."

He promised—in return—to read Boswell's *Johnson,* which, she had only recently discovered, unbelieving, he had never got around to reading; and they walked lazily to her apartment on F Street. "I won't ask you in tonight, Blacky. I've got a dozen papers to grade by 9 A.M."

"See you tomorrow?"

"Sure." They kissed good night, and Blackford decided to walk the twenty blocks to his own apartment.

When he reached the reconverted old residence, which now had four apartments, the doorway was very dark. The streetlight at the corner, on which he generally relied to illuminate the keyhole, was for some reason not functioning. Not having a match, he had to use his fingers to probe the cavity. After some manipulation, he managed to introduce the key that opened the door. Normally he could flick on the hall light, and turn it off at the top of the stairs—nothing, literally nothing, enraged Mrs. Carstairs more than when one of her three tenants left the hall light on, and she had been known to conduct more than one summary court-martial to establish whether it was Blackford Oakes, the good-looking young man upstairs who worked for some engineering company or other; or the rear admiral opposite; or, on the ground floor, the deputy director of the Internal Revenue Service. The three men would take turns admitting guilt, knowing that nothing less than a formal finding would satisfy Mrs. Carstairs. It was thus very infrequently, nowadays, that the light was left on.

But tonight the light was on. Reaching the top of the stairwell, Blackford first inserted his apartment key, then turned off the hall light. It was a matter of three or four steps to the lamp switch, whose exact location he knew from extensive experience. Before reaching it, he sensed that the room was occupied. He drew breath, grabbed the lamp with both hands to use it if necessary as a bludgeon, and with his rump, turned on the wall switch. Seated in a chair opposite was Vadim Platov.

"*Goddam it,* Vadim!" Blackford restored the lamp to its position on the table. "Why in the hell did you have to spook your way in here? You could have sent me a—postcard."

"Blackford"—for the first time, Blackford heard Vadim Platov refer to him other than as "Julian." "I went through many pains to find you."

"I hope so."

"I used up, to the brim, all of my resources. I could not risk not having you see me, and you know, I am, under the contract with the—firm—not permitted into Washington, I break my own security arrangements, and of course finding you, I break others, but the cause is necessary; it is the most necessary cause of my life."

"Okay, Vadim, okay. Let me get you something from the kitchen. What would you like?"

"Some tea."

Blackford knew the problem must be grave. He put on the kettle, with its screeching device to call when the water boiled, brought in a pot with tea bags and two glasses, milk and sugar, took off his gabardine jacket, and sprawled on the couch. "What's up?"

Vadim withdrew an envelope from his wallet, and handed it to Blackford, who examined first the face of it, which revealed no sender's name or return address. The letter, addressed to "Anton Sokolin" at a post-office box in central New York State, had been airmailed from Stockholm on the first of September and received by Vadim on September 4. He opened it. The message was written in German on airmail stationery, in the meticulous script of a patient writer working in a foreign language. Blackford read it slowly.

> Dear Mr. Sokolin:
> I am advised by Tamara, whose message reached me through channels I have every reason to believe were intercepted, that only you and possibly an American named Julian can prevent the scheduled execution of her husband, my brother Viktor. The circumstances are not described why this should be so, and under the cir-

cumstances I have no explanation to make. Tamara tells me that unless you and Julian make available to one B-o-l-g-i-n [she separated the letters of the name with hyphens] that element which Viktor's patrons require in order to "consummate their enterprise"—her words exactly—Viktor will be executed. Already he has been tortured. They are kept apart, and Tamara does not therefore know how much he suffers. But the message, she says, is inescapably clear: Mr. Bolgin must have the information by September 10, or my brother will be dead. No words of mine, added to those of Tamara, can move you more than this message, unadorned. I do not know what is at stake, other than the life of my beloved Viktor, who has already suffered too much. And I know from the past that you shared his torment and saved him once. Yours prayerfully,

The letter was signed simply, "Vera."

Blackford was summoned by the keening of the tea kettle. His mind was blurred with thought, anger, frustration, and his movements were entirely mechanical. He poured the tea as a robot might have done. "Sugar? . . . milk?" He paced back and forth. Vadim stirred his tea nervously. He looked very old, his broad shoulders seemed shrunken, and in his eyes the vitality of Paris was gone. There was a look there of fatalism, and trust. For minutes, neither spoke.

Blackford sat down. "So they fooled us. Did you know they *actually* handed over the shipment of arms to the Algerians?"

"Perhaps by then they did not know. Besides, Rufus's Algerian contacts boarded the *Chekhov* maybe before Viktor appeared."

Of course, Blackford thought. Stupid! What had happened, obviously, was that they had tortured Viktor. But why? What had he done or said that made them suspicious?

"Do you know what they want, Vadim?"

"Yes, Julian. I mean, Blackford."

Blackford looked up at him. *"How* do you know?"

"Because you told me. That morning, when we were both interrogating Viktor. It was before lunch, you remember, you were finishing with reading over your notebook and you . . . you were checking it to see if you asked all the questions your American scientist told you about asking, and it was then you read on with the notes, and you told me about—the Van de Graaff."

Blackford looked hard at Vadim.

"Vadim, it's the middle of the night of September 9. This letter was received in Tivoli, New York, on September 4. That's five days ago. It took you five days to find me?"

"No, Julian. I am older than you, and sometimes breath-short, and your whereabouts are not being advertised, but it does not take me five days to find you, when Viktor's life is hanging on the balance."

"So?"

Vadim looked down, forlorn.

"In five days," he said, "I traveled to London and back. I met with Colonel Bolgin—we grew up in the same town, it happens—there was time for the little talk, too."

Blackford grew impatient. "Time for small talk *during what?*"

"During the period when he waited for Moscow's answer."

"Moscow's answer to what?"

"To whether they would release Viktor and Tamara if I gave them the secret for the transistors."

Blackford jumped up from his chair. "What did they say?"

"They said yes."

"All right, Vadim. Details. Details. Details."

"Very well, Julian. I tell you this because I have sworn great love for America. I am telling you something I should not be telling you *until tomorrow night.*"

"What happens tomorrow night?"

Vadim looked instinctively at his watch. "By tomorrow night, two things happen. If by three P.M. eastern daylight time the Russian freighter leaves the American port with the Van de Graaff, Viktor and Tamara will be on the eleven P.M. Moscow-time nonstop SAS flight, Moscow to Stockholm."

Blackford was unbelieving. "But you tell me this tonight. When there is still time to stop the freighter, wherever it is." A test, he thought suddenly: "Where is it?"

The reply was instantaneous. "Portsmouth, New Hampshire."

"What is its name?"

"The *Mechta.*"

"When is the Van de Graaff scheduled to load?"

"Tomorrow, about noon."

It was fatally clear to Blackford. Vadim had, calmly, handed

Blackford the hand grenade. If it went off, Viktor would die. Vadim had left it to Blackford to decide whether to act now, or wait twenty-four hours, when it would be too late to stop the shipment.

"What do you *expect* me to do, Platov? I'm not the goddam U.S. Government. I'm not even God! I only work here. We mounted a huge operation, at tremendous risk, to capture the headlines, restore morale, and reassure the whole tired, sick, hopeless world that we're *still* number one, and cheer them and give them hope. We succeeded. Or we think we're on the way to succeeding. Now you're asking *me* to lie low—"

"Only for twenty-four hours."

"—to lie low and risk the whole shebang, possibly the lives of millions. In order to save the life of one Russian."

"Viktor is more than one Russian."

"Why?"—Blackford almost shouted it out.

"He is, first of all, Viktor Kapitsa, the gentlest man of science ever born. Second, he is," and it was Vadim's turn to raise his voice, *"the man who gave you the Russian secrets you desperately needed."*

"Vadim, Vadim, look. My experience with Viktor was over three days, in a comfortable villa. Yours was over eight years, in hell. Even in three days I came to know that Viktor—and Tamara—were special. And my whole point about the operation is really the same as yours. *Viktor* gave us what we wanted. But the fact that *he* gave it to us shouldn't mean that it's suddenly valueless! Shouldn't mean that there was *no point* in our breaking our ass to get it. What you're asking is that we *reverse the whole business*. To spare Viktor's life. But we *risked* Viktor's life in the first place—and he was willing to do it. The logic is airtight. Viktor cooperated with us, he *gave* us what we wanted because *he knew* it was important for us to have it. For us, now, to give it back is to undo not only our own thinking but also Viktor's thinking. *Don't you follow me?"*

"You speak like a lawyer."

"No. I don't. I speak like a goddam philosopher. A transideological philosopher. It was Trotsky who said, 'Who says A must say B.' Viktor said A. Tell me: Why didn't Viktor defect?"

"Because, he told me, he does not think he could live outside Russia. I understand that feeling also. Sometimes I am so miserable with homesickness."

Blackford said nothing. How did what Vadim said change the bargain? Viktor's life in return for: the first satellite?

Vadim spoke again. "I need not tell you, Blackford, that I would kill myself before telling to anybody that I visited you tonight. I had to tell you, because my conscience it is not big enough for the heavy load. Tomorrow night I will telephone to confess. I will telephone to the Director. I will tell him—unless you interrupt my plans—that it is—done. By then, Viktor will be flying to Stockholm. He—after he reports to the President—they—will have to decide themselves whether—*Mechta* reaches Sebastopol."

"Where are you staying, Vadim?"

"I am going to drive back to my house tonight."

"It's one in the morning, and you live on the Hudson."

"I will not sleep until eleven P.M., Moscow time, tomorrow. If you send the police to stop the shipment, why do I need to be here to know about it? I will be in my house maybe at noon, maybe earlier."

Vadim got up and, dejectedly, walked toward the door. He reached for Blackford's hand perfunctorily, and then he broke down, his arms around the taller man, sobbing, his whole frame shaking. Blackford returned the embrace, and said soothingly, again and again, "I'll see, Vadim, I'll see, Vadim. I'll see. . . ."

* * *

The following day, September 10, at ten in the morning, on the ground floor of an office building in a suburb of Boston, a trim middle-aged man wearing a double-breasted suit, an unsullied raincoat, and a brown fedora, and carrying a slim leather briefcase, scanned the directory, and then entered the elevator, depressing the ninth-floor knob. He went to 912, on the entrance pane of which was lettered, *High Voltage Engineering Corporation*. He presented his card to the receptionist, who excused herself, and presently beckoned him to follow her to the office of Mr. Arrowsmith.

Arrowsmith rose, and extended his hand. "So nice to see you, Mr. Gautier. Can I take your coat?"

Gautier allowed the comptroller to remove it. He sat down opposite the desk, and opened his briefcase. He spoke with a French accent.

"I have here, Monsieur Arrowsmith, as we arranged over the telephone yesterday, a certified check in the amount of $210,000 drawn on the Bank of Montreal, for your unit, which I understand you can make available to me immediately at your warehouse?"

"Yes, indeed. It is assembled. The technicians worked on it late into the night. I am delighted your company has found use for it. It is a very versatile machine. I believe we have three units in operation in Canada, so yours will hardly be the first!"

"Indeed. But we hope our products will be the best . . . in the whole world."

"What exactly does your company produce, if I may ask, Mr. Gautier?"

"I shall be very happy to send you our literature. Perhaps—who knows—you will one of these days be purchasing something from us?"

"Who knows, indeed, who knows," said Arrowsmith, writing out a receipt. "Young John from this office will take you to the warehouse. You have your own van, you said?"

"It is waiting outside."

"Fine, then—here's your receipt." He rang a buzzer, and an ill-kempt, fat seventeen-year-old, chewing gum, came in. "This is my son John. John, Monsieur Gautier from Canada. You're to show him the way to the warehouse. Give this"—he handed a slip to John—"to Phil Kemp. He'll take it from there." Mr. Arrowsmith looked at the large clock on the wall. "I figure you should be back in the office not later than eleven, John." Gautier looked aside rather than appear to take notice of an exercise in paternal discipline. "Good-bye, Monsieur Gautier. Or is there anything else I can do for you while you're in Burlington?"

"Thank you, no. I'll carry my raincoat. Thank you, and good-bye."

An hour later the van was loaded. It required six men to ease the cumbersome machine into it. The foreman, Phil Kemp, handed a bulky work manual to Gautier. "Sorry we don't have one of these in French."

"No problem," Gautier said. "Our people can handle English without any trouble."

"Okay, then, good luck with it."

They shook hands.

Two hours later the van was at the wharf in Portsmouth, New Hampshire, where the ship was docked. The men and hauling machines were ready. It was the work of forty-five minutes to remove the Van de Graaff unit to the loading platform, lift it up over the deck, lower it into the belly of the ship, and secure it. By three in the afternoon, the snap of autumn in the air coming in with a fresh northeasterly, the freighter was cleared by the harbormaster to leave the port. Promptly the Russian freighter *Mechta* loosened its dock lines and set out on the planned fourteen-day passage to Sebastopol.

Chapter 28

"MR. PRESIDENT, might I make a procedural suggestion?"

The President glowered, but said nothing. That meant yes.

"It's just this. The question what to do with Serge, or what to do *to* him, we can take as long as we want to decide. He's not going anyplace. He's desperate, all right, but if there's any extreme we could classify as possible, it's that he might commit suicide, as an act of repentance. Or more properly, atonement. After all, he told *me* what he did. And Serge is solely responsible. If he didn't have a troubled conscience, we wouldn't know now that the Van de Graaff is on its way to Russia. The point is, he's not going to leave that little house of his on the Hudson. He's not going to fly the coop. So if your instructions are to throw the book at him, we can do that—tomorrow, a week from tomorrow, or a month from tomorrow. There's only one question on a short fuse, and that is: Do we, or don't we, stop the *Mechta?*"

The President, having expressed himself vigorously on Communists, defectors, scientists, intelligence services, counterintelligence services, defective security, and general brainlessness, was suddenly: the commander in chief. He turned to the Secretary of State:

"On a scale of zero to one hundred"—it was one of the President's favorite formulations, and everyone in the Situation Room—the Secretary, the Director, the chairman of the Joint Chiefs, the chief of Naval Operations, the national security advisor—had heard him use it again and again: "on that scale, where would you put a satellite launch by the Soviet Union ahead of one by our own people?"

"I would put it, Mr. President, at one hundred. I can't think of a single accomplishment by the Soviet Union with greater potential impact. To travel, in the public memory, in one year, from the country that gunned down Hungarian students to the country that launched a space program, with the obvious implications this has of a military nature, is an exercise in self-transformation. The neutralists arrange their moral priorities with their eye on power. That is my judgment of the matter."

The President turned to his national security advisor. "You agree, Bob?"

"Yes, I do. Even though I assume within one year we would overtake them. The legend is that all important Soviet scientific postwar achievements—the atom bomb, the hydrogen bomb, the whole works—are derivative. In a way, that's true. But Tsiolkovsky, the major theorist of rocket flight, was after all a Russian. The point is they've developed a forward inertia, and a space satellite would give it explosive credibility, shifting world opinion, critically, in the neutralist world especially. I have here something written by Whittaker Chambers after the Russian ICBM tests were announced a couple of weeks ago. Listen to one sentence: 'Before this illimitable prospect'—he's talking about Russian scientific advances in missiles—'humility of mind might seem the beginning of reality of mind. As starter, we might first disabuse ourselves of that comforting, but, in the end, self-defeating notion that Russian science, or even the Communist mind in general, hangs from treetops by its tail.'"

"Hm. That feller can sure write. Why don't we get him to work up some speeches for me? Talk to Nixon about that, Bob. Yeah, I see your point. Now answer me something else: If we stop the *Mechta,* how long do you suppose it would be before they got themselves another one of those machines? I take it there are three hundred or whatever around, and that they're not even on the banned-export list—nobody at Commerce was told about the sensitivity of the goddam thing—"

"Mr. President," the Director said gently but firmly, "we didn't want to advertise in any way that it had a potential security value..."

"Yeah, yeah. There's always a *reason*. But back to the question: Suppose we clamped a security ban on export, and regulated production and sales, how long would we hold 'em up?"

The chairman of the Joint Chiefs spoke up. "We've looked into that question, sir, and it's hard to say. We figure to go with our launch in January. If we could hold the Russians three-four months, that would make the difference. They're not likely to find an alternative to the E-beam Van de Graaff system—"

"Don't get scientific with me, Nate."

"Sorry, sir. I mean, they're not likely to find another way around the problem they've got left. They know now the *existence* of the machine. Allen will have the exact location of every unit by noon tomorrow, as I understand it. With three hundred of them sitting around, a total of eight abroad, the best we could hope for is keeping them out of Russia for six months or so."

"Six months would do it?"

"Yes, sir."

"So what you're all saying boils down to this: If we stop the *Mechta, we'll* launch the first satellite. Is there a simpler way of saying it? The Washington *Post* is always saying I'm a simpleton, which I may be, if it takes a simpleton to understand that if the Washington *Post* was running the country we'd be broke, invaded, or both, in six months. Make that eight months. Anyway, is that too simple a way to put it?"

There was silence in the room.

"Okay, now if we decided to pull her in... Where is she right now, Arleigh?"

The chief of Naval Operations replied:

"At 1700, the *Mechta* was 450 miles east of Portsmouth, on a course of 075 degrees, leaving her, as it happens, exactly 2,500 miles from Gibraltar. She's traveling at sixteen knots, 384 miles per day, so she would reach Gibraltar in the early morning of the eighteenth."

"What've you got tailing her?"

"Two submarines, two U-2's, two destroyers, one cruiser."

"And standing by?"

"We could get any aircraft over her within two hours, the

cruiser and the destroyer within five hours. The subs are on her tail right now."

"What alternatives have you considered?" The President rather liked conversations of this nature. Less than totally organized in his own verbal enterprises, he enjoyed precision in others; absent prolixity.

"Well, sir, the question is of course political. Militarily, we can do anything you tell us to do. We can apprehend the *Mechta,* we can sink it, we can cripple it. I think, actually, that exhausts the possibilities."

"I should think that would," the Secretary commented. "Unless you want to admit a fourth hypothetical possibility, which is to parachute Billy Graham down, convert the captain, and have him steer the boat back to Portsmouth."

"Why do you go and pick on Billy Graham?" the President said. "He's a sincere individual, and I like him. Foster, you're the last Puritan."

"Not if our foreign policy is successful, Mr. President. In that event there will be more Puritans."

The President chuckled. "Okay. Let's think a bit about the possibility of an accident. Seems to me, if the *Andrea Doria* can bump into the *Stockholm* in broad daylight off Nantucket, one of our young pilots might run into the *Mechta* in the middle of the night, no? Any wop pilots on those destroyers?"

"We'd have to proceed on the understanding that the Soviet Union would know right away it wasn't an accident," the Director said.

"Of course! Goddam it, Allen, I wish you'd remind yourself every now and then that I had a little to do with winning a world war. I can see the *obvious* things. Tell me things that *aren't* obvious."

"Sorry, Mr. President. Let's go on: The Soviet Union would know we did it intentionally, but they very likely wouldn't announce the motive. In reclamation damages, they wouldn't get to take the deposition of our people on the bridge if we pleaded *nolo contendere*—we do not contest—"

"I know what *nolo contendere* means," the President snapped. "That's what Billy Mitchell did, wasn't it?"

"Well not exactly, sir," the chief of Naval Operations said, but before explaining, he was cut off.

"Never mind. So we get three or four men, the captain of the cruiser and two or three others. What instructions do we give them?"

The Director spoke. "I'm afraid we'd have to sink her. If we merely crippled her, you'd have a Soviet vessel in the act within twenty-four hours taking over the towing operation, and another one scooting off with . . . precious cargo."

"Yes. Well. How easy is it to sink a vessel the size of the *Mechta?*"

"She's nine thousand tons, sir, C-3 class freighter, 410 feet. I should think if we came in on her quarter at an acute angle, at a speed of say twenty knots, you'd gash off her rear end without serious risk to the cruiser."

"Casualties?"

"At midnight there wouldn't be much going on, couple men on the bridge amidships. I don't know where the crew's quarters are. Probably the layout is conventional, and the after end is reserved for engine and cargo. Conceivably we could carry it off without casualties."

The President looked about him. "Anybody want to add anything?" He stood up, and everyone in the Situation Room rose simultaneously.

There was silence.

"Arleigh, deploy to sink the *Mechta* during the midnight hours tomorrow, subject to hearing again from me. Foster, please be here for breakfast tomorrow at eight."

They filed out of the room. The secretaries who had been detained for late work if necessary heard the President discussing with the Secretary of State a certain stiffness in his golf stroke since the ileitis operation. The Secretary attempted to direct the discussion to his own physical ailments, but the President, as they entered the elevator, was still talking about ileitis as a handicap.

Chapter 29

"I KNOW IT'S LATE, and I'm sorry. It's this simple: I have to see you. I can go to you, or if you prefer I'll send a car."

"Hm," the former Secretary pondered. "Better send for me. Alice has guests, and it would be less awkward to leave the house than to remove myself from the party to another room."

"Sorry."

"Don't worry. Crises are the routine of governments."

A half hour later he climbed out of a black car still dressed in black tie. The Director opened the door and led him into the study, where his guest sat down in the usual armchair, while the Director walked over to his studio bar. "What will you have, Dean?"

"Nothing."

"I'm going to have a whiskey. It's been one hell of a day." He put down his pipe, mixed a scotch and soda, cut a piece of cheese from the platter, stuck a couple of crackers on the plate, and walked back and sank down deep in the armchair opposite.

He sipped from the drink, and said: "Here's where we are." Instinctively he looked at his watch. "The Russians got hold of one of those E-beam machines I talked to you about." He raised his hand to deflect the question. "Hold up on how they got it. They *got* it, and it is steaming toward Sebastopol, if you want to know exactly, at sixteen knots, course 075 degrees, five hundred miles out to sea, and present intentions are to sink it."

"To *what?* I'll have a brandy."

The Director returned with the snifter. "My formulation was theatrical and I apologize. The intentions are indeed to sink it, but to make it appear to be an accidental collision at sea."

"Have you arranged for a suitable iceberg?"

"Dean, Dean. *A United States cruiser has been designated to effect the collision.* It is apparently practical and might even be done without loss of life. The Soviet Union would know, of course; but the chance they'd make the accusation publicly is, by the general reckoning, including my own, small. The whole glorious idea of a Soviet satellite is that it's one hundred percent Russian. Not something cannibalized from American bits and pieces. Do you agree they wouldn't go public with it?"

The former Secretary paused. "I agree. They would, however, almost certainly retaliate. That is their mode. They might draw the noose again on Berlin. They might pick up one or two of our people, maybe even more, in Russia, or in Eastern Europe, and do an espionage trial. I doubt they'd sink a U.S. cargo vessel. They don't normally come up with asymmetrical responses, but in this case I think they would. Make it absolutely clear to me: What's in it for us?"

"As far as we can tell, what's in it for us is what we've been after throughout this whole operation: the first satellite, and all that signifies about strategic missile capability and other countries' belief in us."

"Theirs would follow soon?"

"Theirs would certainly follow. How soon we can't say. Anywhere from two to six months later would be my guess."

The former Secretary twirled his glass. "Talk to me about Khrushchev."

"Khrushchev is now pretty much the whole ball game, but he leaned heavily on the military to get there, especially on Zhukov, who would like a fresh war with breakfast every day. Khrushchev is hot-tempered, wily, ambitious, ruthless—but, we have reason to believe, cautious. Anybody who survived Stalin has gifts of guile, and caution."

The Secretary held his snifter to his lips without tilting it. After an interval he said, "Here's what bugs me at that end. If they had simply *stolen* our machine, we had *caught* them in the act, and then had *sunk* the ship that was carrying it away, their reciprocal gesture would tend to be formalistic. But in this situation *we're* the aggressors. *We* abducted a Soviet scientist and got the fruit of Soviet research from him."

"Remember, he gave it to us: We didn't torture it out of him, or anything like that."

"A nice distinction. But not one that Khrushchev would be likely to dwell upon. As far as he's concerned, the satellite technology developed by Russians is Russian property—and *we* took it. Whatever professional admiration he may have for the *way* you got it, he is unlikely to be mollified. How did they find out about the scientist?"

"We don't know. Torture, I suppose. We were given no reason to believe they didn't buy the whole Algerian cover. Hell, they delivered a shipful of arms to Algeria! But anyway, what then happened—to back up—is that *our* old Russian defector got word they were going to string up his old friend, so *he himself* told them about the machine, and where they could get one—which they promptly did, and loaded it on a Soviet freighter."

The former Secretary whistled. "Ah well. We shouldn't be surprised when men act on emotion."

It occurred to the Director that, in another setting, he'd have commented that no doubt the defector took the position that he would not turn his back on his old friend in Russia. "Never mind him, though you can imagine what life was like when Ike was told a Russian defector in the United States turned over to the Communists our principal technological secret—but to go back: I agree. The Soviets would look about for retaliatory opportunities. And hell, there's no way of predicting where they'd act or how. We need to speculate on the probable ferocity of their response—"

"Hold that for a minute, Allen. Let's suspend that, and think domestic for a moment. Now I'm going to tell you something that's been on my mind, gnawing away, since the election. It has a very direct bearing . . ."

He rose and clasped his hands behind his back, a posture habitual with him when lecturing presidents, judges, congressmen, students, or grandchildren.

"In my judgment, the domestic mood is dangerously flabby. Hungary proved that. If I may say so without offending you, your brother's rhetoric, going back to 1952, is now either not heard at all or confined to rallies at the American Legion, and dismissed as rodomontade. Now up to a point I personally welcome this: I am, I suppose, one of the architects of the doctrine of coexistence. What I do *not* welcome is something I fear is happening. And," he sighed rather self-consciously, "it is happening within the womb of my own party."

"The party of brains . . ."

"Precisely. And precisely because it is the party of brains, its strategic consequences are the more to be feared. What is happening is the crystallization of a blend of superiority-and-disengagement, based on the assumption that because we have hydrogen bombs we can drop on Moscow, we are safe. Never mind Hungary. Never mind—when you come right down to it—Berlin: people and places that can't be saved with hydrogen weapons.

"Now"—he lifted his hand to protest any interruption—"I am not saying that attitude has prevailed among thoughtful Democrats. I say it is inchoate in the writings, the attitudes, the acts, of some extremely influential Democrats and not a few Republicans— you saw what they almost did to the military budget? In the Senate, *and* in the House? It took everything Ike could throw at them to get it stitched together again. There is a kind of post-World War, post-Korean, post-Wilsonian languor. Never mind the editorial thunder; it can't *really* be said that the public—or the intellectuals—were *deeply* moved by the Hungarian repression. That same lethargy wafted the whole Suez venture, however misbegotten in the first place, into nothingness. What this country needs is one hell of a jolt, and I'm here to tell you that under the circumstances, a satellite might very well be the kindest thing that ever happened to us. A Soviet satellite." Again he raised his hand to keep from being interrupted. But the Director was merely staring at him. For a moment both men were silent. The former Secretary resumed, "Obviously it would be different if in that little Russian freighter we had packaged an entire intercontinental ballistics technology. But we *know*—you *told* me—what advances they've made, advances we can't undo by one sinking in the North Atlantic. That fact hasn't entered the U.S. consciousness." Again, there was a silent moment. "Why not let them go ahead and wake us up by firing their blasted satellite?"

After a third silence, the Director spoke. "You make the point very well. But you leave out, don't you, the factor of world opinion? I am, as you know, as liberated as any man in America from the usual cant about world opinion. But at certain levels it is an overwhelming palpable force, and nobody knows that better than you. You created NATO. It was do-able only because these people felt the need and the comparable size of our muscle. Can we survive a Soviet satellite?"

"I don't deny the event would shock. I deny that anything that would immediately issue from the event would have conclusive strategic consequences. By contrast, a continued erosion of American resolution, sheltered by technological complacency, would inevitably show up in those little hard encounters three, four, five years from now. I would rather, I am saying, take the jolt now and recover than continue in the direction I think we're headed."

The Director drew a deep breath. The two men sat sipping for a moment.

The former Secretary rose. "Allen, think it over. Call me at any hour. Indeed, perhaps I should leave it that I will expect a call from you before dawn tomorrow. I'll come back, or you can come to me; or, if there is nothing more to discuss, we'll leave it at that."

The Director stood and clasped his friend's hand. "Foster's having breakfast with the President. I'll have a prebreakfast breakfast with Foster."

"Has the President made up his mind?"

"I would say that his mind has been made up subject to its being dramatically reversed."

"Is your mind made up?"

"I hear what you say, Dean. Good night."

Chapter 30

THE RADIO OFFICER wrote down the message in the special code and whistled at its length. It was unusual for Washington to use the Captain's Code; indeed he could remember only a single other occasion when it had been done, and that turned out to have been the prelude to the Inchon landing, seven years earlier in Korea. Well, he figured, that's what captains are for. He dialed 001.

The telephone rang on the desk of Y. Upsilon Jones, who was reading *Forever Amber,* and wondering whether the current mission, whatever it would prove to be, could conceivably take longer than it would take him to get through the book since he read slowly. "Charlie Stagg, sir. There's a long message from CINCLANT in Captain's Code. Shall I bring it down?"

"Yup."

He hid his novel in the desk drawer, and pulled out the most recent volume of Samuel Eliot Morison's naval history of World War II. A long cable in the special code . . . He wasn't all that surprised. Since receiving, a day before, instructions to change course and head 080 degrees, with no further explanation, he had been expecting clarification. There was a knock on the door.

"Come in."

Warrant Officer Charles Stagg, wearing a navy shirt, the sleeves rolled up, and light blue gabardine pants, opened the door, recoiling instinctively at the thick cigar smoke inevitably associated with Captain Y. Upsilon Jones. The captain turned in his revolving chair, title page of his book conspicuous. Puffing on his cigar, he put the book aside and reached for the envelope.

"A long one, eh Charlie?"

"Several hundred words, sir. You don't suppose there's been a coup d'etat and General Curtis LeMay has overthrown the President?"

The captain looked up frostily at the radio officer and blew smoke in his general direction. "Obviously, the communication is intended only for higher authority."

"Yes, sir," said Stagg. "Will that be all?"

"That will be all."

Captain Jones went to the wall safe but then realized he had to start all over again. He had forgotten the combination number. Never mind. He had written it down in the Bible, right by the Ten Commandments, where he knew he could remember to look. He went to his little bookshelf, brought out the Bible, thumbed through Exodus, and saw the little penciled numbers, which would mean nothing to any stranger who happened to find himself in the private quarters of Captain Y. Upsilon Jones, aboard the *Indianapolis,* reading Exodus in the Bible. 5 . . . 26 . . . 21 . . . 5. Once upon a time he had tried to commit the sequence to memory, and although he had done poorly at math at Annapolis, he had devised a little mnemonic aid, based on the difference between 26 and 21 being 5, or something of the sort—he couldn't bother to recall. Above the 5, he had sketched in a tiny arrow pointing to the right, which was to remind him that he should turn the knob clockwise when beginning. Four turns clockwise past 0 ending at 5, three turns counterclockwise past 0 ending at 26, two turns clockwise past 0 ending at 21, one turn counterclockwise past 0 ending at . . . 5. The safe door clicked open, and he reached for the black leather book, sat down, opened it, and looked down the mimeographed table to September 12. Opposite it was written IZN. On another page he found, and jotted down, the corresponding keys. He was left with an alphabetic sequence with which he now painfully wrestled. A pity he couldn't have Charlie do it, because Charlie had a way with codes. After a few minutes, he would have memorized that on this day, an "i" represented a "b," and an "a" represented an "n," and within five minutes he'd be writing out the message almost at dictation speed. But Uppy Jones had to keep referring back to the master code, and it was eleven before he had finished. He reread it whole in stupefaction and then dialed 002 for Joe Jenks, his executive officer. Jenks did not answer, so he bawled out on the general communication system: "Commander Jenks! This is the captain! Report immediately to my quarters." After putting down the microphone he wondered whether that had been wise. Was there an edginess in his voice? There was a hell of a lot to be edgy about. Had Washington gone out of its fucking mind? If only they had somebody at the White House with a solid military background. Suddenly he remembered that, in fact, the incumbent President *did* have a solid military background. No doubt one of those Harvard kooks in there giving him this wild idea—the knock on the door was peremptory.

"Come in."

"What's up, Uppy?"

Silently, Captain Jones handed his subordinate the penciled transcription of the message. Jenks began reading it while standing, but slowly eased himself down in the chair alongside the captain's.

The message began with the Eyes Only Top Secret Immediate Action coding reserved for what they called, at the National Staff and Command School, "decisive actions."

The message read: "YOUR MISSION IS TO SINK NINE THOUSAND TON RUSSIAN FREIGHTER MECHTA AT MOMENT OF YOUR CHOOSING BETWEEN 0300 AND 0400 GMT TOMORROW FRIDAY SEPTEMBER 13. THE MECHTA WILL BE AT APPROXIMATELY LATITUDE 45° 11′ NORTH LONGITUDE 50° 47′ WEST. TRAVELING AT 087 DEGREES SPEED 16 KNOTS. THE SINKING IS TO BE EFFECTED BY MEANS OF COLLISION. IMPERATIVE THE MECHTA GO DOWN BEFORE DAWN. EFFECT OPERATION WITH MINIMUM CASUALTIES. RESTRICT KNOWLEDGE OF YOUR MISSION TO FEWEST PERSONNEL FEASIBLE AND PLEDGE THEM TO SECRECY. SUCCESS OF OPERATION VITAL TO NATIONAL INTEREST. DEVISE APPROPRIATE SUBTERFUGE AND CHECK OUT DETAILS WITH CINCLANT ATTENTION BURKE CODE IZN BY 1500 GMT TODAY." The cable was signed, "CINCLANT BURKE."

Jenks looked up and discerned the gloomy features of the beefy captain through the cigar smoke.

"Mind if I turn on the fan, Uppy?"

"I wouldn't mind if you took command of the whole goddam ship, to tell you the truth."

Joe Jenks, who stayed on in the Navy after the war and had served four years with Jones, knew that the sentiment was wholly sincere. If there was anything Upsilon Jones abhorred more than exercising command, it was the thought of losing it. In two years he would be retired in any case, it having been made clear he would not be promoted. When they gave him the *Indianapolis,* he inherited a prestigious boat and—and Jones knew this—an executive officer who was always there when Jones needed him, which was whenever there was anything to do that required a little coordination. It was not true, as a classmate at Annapolis had once been heard to remark, that Uppy Jones couldn't pilot a boat through the Strait of Gibraltar without hitting either Africa or Spain. But Jones was no Horatio Hornblower, and it suddenly occurred to Joe Jenks that under the circumstances this was providential. He had better be formal for a minute:

"Well, Captain. How do you want to proceed?"

Jones took a deep draft from his cigar.

"I want to proceed by proceeding to assign you the task of working out the details of this dumb-ass assignment."

"All right, Uppy. Let me go back to my quarters, try to think up something, and try it out on you."

"When?"

"An hour?"

"Not later."

"Yes, sir."

* * *

At Washington, in the Situation Room of the Pentagon, the chief of Naval Operations, the chairman of the Joint Chiefs, and the Director of the Central Intelligence Agency looked at the long cable, which they passed one to another.

The Director, who was the last man to read it, looked up at the stern face of the chairman. Since neither of the military men had spoken, the Director broke silence. "I like it."

"So do I," said the chairman of the Joint Chiefs.

"So do I," said the chief of Naval Operations.

The chief of Naval Operations picked up the telephone and reached his deputy. "Jim, cable the *Indianapolis:* 'YOUR PLAN APPROVED. GOOD LUCK.' "

The Director said, "It's pretty ingenious. Who is the captain of the *Indianapolis,* Arleigh?"

"Fellow called Y. Upsilon Jones. Happens to be the biggest asshole in the Navy. It's too good to be true that *he's* going to be the guy who ran into a Russian merchant in the middle of the Atlantic. Oh, the plan? That would be the work of his exec. Jenks. Smart feller."

* * *

There were four men sitting in the little office of the captain. Jenks had what amounted to a director's script in his hand.

"All right, we'll go over it. 'X' designates the moment of impact. Just how many minutes and seconds after 0300 X will take place is a decision that will be made approximately ten minutes before X.

"All right. We are at present on a course that should bring the *Mechta* into our radar screen at 0200, possibly earlier. We will have turned 180 degrees, to head west, one hour earlier, so that we'll be approaching the *Mechta* bow to bow.

"At 0300"—he turned to Lieutenant J. G. Plummer, who looked nineteen years old, and in fact was—"what do you do, Plummer?"

"I tell Walker, who'll be at the helm, to go to my cabin and work out the dawn star positions, that the exercise will be good for him, that I'm feeling a little lazy tonight, and I'll take the helm. I'll instruct Ensign Goodbody, who'll have the CONN, to go with him and supervise the work. As soon as they've gone down, I'll tell the helmsman, the lee helmsman, and the watch quartermaster to go below—it's a quiet night, and the new watch will be coming along in a few minutes."

"Correct. That will clear the bridge, and the two lookouts forward will be caught up in the general chaos. Now at that point we'll be three miles east of the *Mechta,* one half mile north of it, on a westerly course of 265 degrees. At that point, we will calculate X—the minutes and seconds to impact—and turn off the running lights and the masthead lights.

"At X minus five minutes, I'll begin to reduce the parallel distance between our courses, but always maintaining sufficient distance so as not to alarm the *Mechta*'s radar guy if he happens to be tracking us.

"Charlie, what do you do?"

"I'm at the radio. If there is any sound out of the *Mechta,* anything at all, I start transmitting a continuous Mayday on that channel blocking out their transmission."

"Correct. And if there is no transmission, as I expect there won't be?"

"I stand by the set—until the moment of impact."

"And then?"

"I send out a signal."

"Saying?—and don't forget the foreign accent."

"Saying: CALLING IZ FREIGHTER MECHTA ENNY SHIIP AT SEA. OUWER POHZISHUN—LATITUTE X, LONGITUTE Y. WIITH US ON BOART IZ ILL SAILORR WHOO NEETS EMERGENCY TREETMENT BY DOKTOR RIGHT AWAY. EEF YOU ARE IN REGION AND HAV DOKTOR ON BOART, CALL PLEES. WILL REPEAT . . ."

"Correct. And then?"

"Assuming their radio survives the collision, I'll crowd it out with strong Mayday signals citing position."

"And assuming their radio is knocked out?—which is likelier?"

"I'll report: 'Mayday Mayday Mayday. This is the U.S. naval cruiser *Indianapolis*. Reporting midocean collision with Russian freighter. Freighter foundering. Position, latitude et cetera, longitude et cetera. Request assistance from all ships in area.'"

Jenks turned to Jones:

"Captain, you will sound a general alarm. But from that point on, we'll have to play it by ear."

"I take it I'm at the wheel for the actual ramming, sir?"

"Yes, Plummer. You're not a career officer. We'll all back you up. I'll flash the big beam in time to measure exactly where we want to hit the bugger. That beam will have 'blinded you.' Our story is straightforward. We happened to be a mere half mile from the *Mechta* when we got the distress call. The radio operator gave the message to Plummer. Plummer called me. I told him to head for the ship, I'd be on the bridge right away as soon as I alerted the captain. I rang the captain, then rushed to the bridge, flashed the beam—but we made a fatal misjudgment. Boats in the area will record having overheard a series of radio messages that are sequentially plausible."

Plummer took a deep breath. "Sir, what about the problem of there being no sick man aboard the *Mechta?*"

"That, Plummer, will be an enduring mystery of the sea."

"The Russians are never going to believe this, sir."

"Our job is to satisfy CINCLANT, not Moscow. This plan has been approved. Is that correct, Captain?"

Captain Jones took a deep drag from his cigar. "Better than that. They complimented me on my plan."

Chapter 31

"WHAT'S EATING YOU, BLACKY?" Sally had had enough. During the dinner, which she had taken pains in preparing, and at which he had merely picked, he had gone on and on with an aimless story about a rumored controversy between the White House and the Defense Department. Into the story, Blackford was under the mistaken impression that he had successfully force-fed considerable zest, when in fact his stomach was churning with self-recrimination, doubt, the agony of the hours between midnight the night before when Vadim left him, and midafternoon, during which Blackford had a total of fifteen hours' opportunity to —do his duty. One telephone call. Three words: "Van-de-Graaff . . . Russian-freighter . . . Portsmouth-New-Hampshire." Three words, and? And Viktor Kapitsa would be taken from the Lubyanka, not to the airport, but to the famous cellar, and there, shot. Yes, of course he felt relief at having kept that from happening. But his assignment wasn't to keep Viktor alive *at all costs*. . . . In his mind he went over and over and over the arguments, while jabbering: until Sally abruptly put an end to it.

"I'm sorry, darling. I'm distracted," he responded.

"Do you want to tell me?"

"*No.*"

He was surprised by the apparent harshness of his rejection. But how could he begin . . . ?

"I mean—I can't. I'd better go, Sally. I'm sorry."

She got up, leaned over, kissed him lightly on the forehead.

Blackford went directly to his apartment and even noticed, with incommensurate relief, that the hall light was not on. He took off shirt and trousers, pulled out the portable Olivetti, and put it on the coffee table. Sitting on his couch, he batted out the letter to Benjamin, Benjamin being his administrative superior at the Central Intelligence Agency: indeed, the only identity within the CIA with whom he was continuously in touch, the others, like Anthony, coming into, and going out of, his life, depending on the assignment.

Dear Benjamin:

I am, beginning today (9/10/57), taking a leave of absence without pay. Inasmuch as I am not engaged in any project at the moment, and am spending my time wheel-spinning, as they *don't* put it in the bureaucracy (I am being ungrateful: in fact I am certainly enjoying, and probably profiting from, the extensive reading list handed to me), I am confident that I can do so without inconveniencing, let alone jeopardizing, the national security. Forgive me my arbitrary behavior, but my reasons are compelling. I expect, on my return, to submit my resignation, but I hope you will agree with me that no purpose would be served by upstreaming (I learned that word in a commercial manual included in the eclectic package assigned to me) my decision, or the reason for it. In particular, I would be disappointed if you felt it necessary to communicate it to Serge, Rufus, or A. Trust. I am going abroad, and cannot be reached. If there are reasons, and I cannot imagine what they could be, why empires might rise or fall depending on whether you can find me, leave word with Sally Partridge, who is the light of my life, and resides at 1775 F; or with my mother, Lady Carol Sharkey, 50 Portland Place, London W1.

With all good wishes,
Blackford

He inserted another sheet of paper into the typewriter:

Dear Sally:

You were right, I am distracted. So much so that I must be off. I don't know for how long, a few weeks, probably. On my return I may have news for you of *profound* meaning for thee and me. If you feel like it, send me a carbon of your review in care of dear old mum, 50 Portland Place, you will recall. I'll check it out for historical and literary solecisms, to ensure that you don't embarrass the future Mrs.——

He signed formally, "Blackford Oakes."

* * *

It was ten o'clock daylight in Washington, midnight local time aboard the *Mechta,* and 0200 in Greenwich. Seaman Second Mate Andrei Vlasov steadfastly maintained a course of 087 degrees steering from a bridge illuminated by three dome lights shining their rays through red-stained glass, the standard cockpit illumination of navigators at sea, and in the air. At his side, seated and working out a crossword puzzle under the port light, was First Officer Tyrkov.

"What's a nine-letter word for a Georgian cheese beginning with T-V?"

Pause. "I'm afraid I wouldn't know, sir," the young sailor replied, which was how he always replied to First Officer Tyrkov, who, for some reason, continued to solicit his help with the puzzles during the tedious midnight watch they shared. The sky was overcast, the temperature outside brisk, but possibly it would clear and there would be stars in the morning. First Officer Tyrkov reflected that the only redeeming feature of this particular watch was that it relieved him of the responsibility of descrying those elusive little stars, which he would have been responsible for doing on the preceding watch, or the succeeding one. Of course—no stars, no sights. They proceeded under dead reckoning, and they could still bring in the Consolan signal from Nantucket, almost a thousand miles away, at 194 kh. In any case, navigation was the least of his concerns while still two thousand miles away from Gibraltar. But Captain Spektorsky was a stickler about these things, the kind of man who would expect you to take star sights astern even if you could actually see the Rock of Gibraltar ahead. First Officer Tyrkov wondered, suddenly, whether there was such a thing as a star-fetishist? Perhaps *that* would explain the captain's obsessive concern with the blasted stars, his drillmaster attitude toward his three watch officers in the matter of the stars, and navigation in general. In which connection, he thought to bestir himself to the starboard side of the bridge, to look at the radar screen. The radar boasted a range of thirty-two miles, but Tyrkov doubted the radar would spot the Himalayan Mountains if they were thirty-two miles away. He found it generally effective, really, only to a range of twenty-five miles. There was in fact a ship out there, eleven degrees north of the *Mechta*'s course, twenty-two miles distant. No way of telling which way the ship was traveling until there was relative movement. He made a notation on the log, and said out loud to Vlasov, "Remind me to check the radar again in five minutes. See where the ship out there—one point off our bow—is headed."

"Yes, sir."

He returned to his crossword puzzle and lit a cigarette. He decided to see if he could penetrate the obdurate intellectual listlessness of Vlasov.

"What's a 'metal,' six letters, the first four S-T-A-L?"

As usual, Vlasov paused—to give the impression that he had strained to find the answer. And then, as usual, "I'm afraid I don't know, sir."

"Don't know! *Idiot!* Have you never heard of *Stalin?* Or did it never occur to you that *steel* was a metal? I am aware, Vlasov, that Stalin has been purged from official party favor, but no directives have come out of the Kremlin—or have I missed any?—decreeing that the metal alloy of which this ship is constructed is from now on going to be called *Khrushchev*."

"Sorry, sir. For some reason I just didn't think."

Tyrkov threw down his pencil. "Tell you what, let's play a quick game of chess. Stick her into automatic steering."

"The captain frowns on that, sir."

"The captain also frowns on insubordination—don't worry, we'll keep our eyes on the course. Which reminds me"—he walked over to the radar screen.

"Hm. Coming in this general direction. Nineteen miles out, still ten, eleven degrees off to port." From under the huge pile of charts in the bottom drawer under the navigation counter he brought out a box, and spread out the chessboard, setting up the players.

"We'll see if you can do any better against me tonight than you did last night." The night before, not feeling sleepy after being relieved, Tyrkov had invited Vlasov into Tyrkov's tiny little cabin, where he kept the vodka. They played a game and shared a half pint.

"Very well, Andrei Petrovich." Vlasov engaged the automatic mechanism, checked to see that the prescribed course was being properly maintained, and then moved the chessboard, dragging over one of the tall stools to perch on.

At 0250 GMT, Tyrkov said: "We'll finish it below, in my cabin. You'd better boil the water now." It was a traditional courtesy of a watch going off duty to boil water so that the watch taking over could set out with hot tea. Vlasov stepped back into the adjacent engineer's compartment where a kettle and an electric range were kept, alongside the little cabinet containing sugar, tea, cups, and a few spoons, while Tyrkov busied himself completing the log. He was still writing when, wearing a cap, a dark sweater, and baggy wool pants, his relief officer arrived, yawning.

"Any action, Andrei Petrovich?"

"No. Still overcast, doubt you'll be seeing the stars, heh heh heh—too bad, old thing. Wind picked up a little, force three from west-southwest, barometer steady."

"Traffic?"

"Yeah. A big mama. And damned if she didn't go by without running lights or a masthead light. I logged her at 0250, heading west by north."

"How far north of our track?"

Tyrkov pored over the log and looked again at the radar screen. "I figure he must have been a half mile off when he went by."

The relief officer went over to the radar. "Yes. She's six miles behind us now. I don't see anything else."

"No, nothing else."

"Anything over the radio?"

"Zilch."

"How did you make out with the crossword puzzle?"

"Awful. S-t-a-l-i-n is no longer a metal. This puzzle book, Lieutenant Popov, will have to be turned in to security when we reach Sebastopol."

Popov laughed, accepting the tea brought in by his helmsman, who looked sleepy.

* * *

Blackford, carrying a briefcase crammed with books and a heavy suitcase, caught the 7 A.M. flight to La Guardia, taxied to Idlewild, and was an hour early for the daily flight to Stockholm. He checked in and read the New York *Herald-Tribune*. He found himself reading the paper back to front, as if to shield himself from the international news. Two books were reviewed. A new writer, Jack Kerouac, had published a book called *On the Road*, and the reviewer hailed it, or, more accurately, taxonomized it, as a "quintessential expression of the rootlessness of the World War II generation," for many of whom sheer movement was a compulsion. Blackford reflected that young Kerouac's habit, as he understood it from the review, was much less expensive than his own. You could hitchhike to San Francisco a lot cheaper than what SAS charged to take you to Stockholm. John Bartlow Martin had completed a six-month tour of the Deep South, and *his* book was called *The Deep South Says Never*. There would never be racial integration of the schools in the South. Blackford hadn't given the subject much thought, though he supposed he should. There had been a Negro tapped for Skull & Bones while he was there, so Yale was ahead of Earl Warren—or behind, if you wanted to take the position of the people John Bartlow Martin had evidently been talking to. He turned impulsively to the front page. Adenauer had won in Germany, with his usual landslide. The General Assembly of the United Nations—what do you know—had condemned the Soviet Union's repression of the Hungarian revolt by 60 to 10 (the Soviet bloc plus Yugoslavia). Jolly good. Theo would like that. And it only took the U.N. ten months.

The flight was called, and he found the tourist section gratifyingly uncrowded, taking a window seat near the rear section of the Constellation. At lunch he ordered a scotch, contrary to his normal noonday habit, and in due course ordered a second. Why did he have to try to see Viktor? Was it to take personal satisfaction from seeing him alive? So what would that establish? Would it prove that he, Blackford, hadn't bloody-well taken U.S. policy into his own hands, disrupted an extensive operation, affected—if he was to believe the validity of the underlying analysis that had taken them all to Paris—history itself: to save Viktor? Yet he knew he had to see him. Perhaps—conceivably?—now that Viktor was permanently out of the Soviet Union, there might be some more useful information he might give Blackford? Which he could carry back to Washington, as a kind of valedictory gift?

Oh, he had had some wild thoughts on Monday night, after Vadim left. It was dawn before Blackford attempted sleep, dawn before he finally reached the excruciating decision to keep silent through the fateful hours during which the machine would be taken from friendly soil to the Russian freighter. Halfway through that bottle of scotch he had nursed a wildly heroic idea. He would go to Spain. He would rent an airplane. Perhaps he could get the use of any army plane at the U.S. base there: He certainly was skilled in manipulating connections. There wasn't a plane in use he couldn't fly after an hour's checkout, given his background in the Air Force. Then he would calculate when the *Mechta* would reach the Strait. He could figure that one out easily enough. That sort of thing was his profession, after all. He could fly out, having got a description of the *Mechta* from the documented merchant marine manuals, and anticipate by several hours its actual arrival at the Strait. Then—then what, Black baby? *Then you might kamikaze your way down into the hold,* is that what you're thinking? To his astonishment that *was* what he was thinking, however briefly. The engineer in him, combined with a certain biological imperative, caused him to think of more . . . platonic means of achieving the same end—say a torpedo? He didn't care *what* his Instant Popularity at the Air Force Base at Torrejón was, he somehow doubted that the commanding officer would say to him: "Here, Blacky, help yourself to a torpedo plane! Here's how you release the actual torpedo . . ." He could, he supposed, devise in time a crude but quite effective bomb which he could drop on the *Mechta* and, with luck, penetrate the deck, or cause an explosion, or contrive in some way to wreck that bloody machine. Or—was it possible that Official America would work something out? Ironic if he were summoned to play a role in such an operation. When he had called Vadim later that night to ask what had been the reaction of the Director when Vadim told him the machine was on a Russian freighter at sea, Vadim said: "He just hung up." It was during that terse conversation with Vadim that Blackford had wrested from him the name and address of Viktor's sister in Stockholm. Though Vadim had sworn he would never give it out, he now tendered it to Blackford in dumb gratitude for his silence during that critical morning. Blackford didn't tell him he planned to go to Stockholm, and the conversation was brief, dribbling off with Vadim going on about how perhaps the Russians would not be able to master the machine in time. Blackford could not be harsh with him. He was hardly in a position to be harsh, though there was a kind of derivative cowardice, he thought, in Vadim's having shared the secret with him. But the weight had been too much for Vadim's shoulders. And, anyway, how could one stay angry with someone like Vadim? Who had experienced what Vadim had experienced? Blackford had simply wanted to terminate the conversation, and so he said, "Yes, Vadim. Maybe somebody will think of something. Let's hope so."

It was dawn in Stockholm when after twelve hours the Constellation eased down over the calm blue-black bays and grassy estuaries approaching the city. Blackford had not slept, and although he had selected a book advertised as a "page-turner"—horrible expression, he thought—and had dutifully turned the pages, reaching the last chapter he could not recall what it was that happened in the first chapter—which was something like finding the key after losing the lock. Especially inasmuch as the last chapter provided the key to what had happened in the first. He didn't feel particularly tired—it was after all only 10 P.M. at home—but even in Stockholm there wasn't much action at dawn; so he went to the Lord Nelson Hotel, where they had his reservation. In his room, he showered, reread Chapter One of his thriller, and went to sleep.

He woke at noon, ordered coffee, put on khaki pants, and sat at the desk, where he wrote:

Dear Tamara:

I cannot predict your reaction to hearing from me. It seems another age when I picked you and Viktor up in the taxicab. I was, in a way, instrumental in causing you and Viktor terrible pain and misery. I have, in a way not by any means honorable (given the priority of my official concerns) attempted to make it up to you and Viktor, with whom I feel a great need to talk. I can tell you upon my honor that I have advised not a single person that I came to Stockholm. My visit is entirely unofficial. I shall wait at the hotel until I hear from you.

Yours faithfully,
Julian

P.S. You will infer, correctly, that I got the address of your sister-in-law from Vadim. When you hear why he broke his word in giving it to me, I think you will not reproach him for it.

He called the concierge and asked him to send up someone who would deliver a letter, and he gave the street address. "How far away is that?"

"Oh, about fifteen minutes, not more."

"Thank you."

Ten or fifteen minutes. He rang for the floor waiter to order lunch as he worked out the possibilities. The first was that she would receive the letter, pick up the telephone, and call him back right away. A second was that she would read the letter and resolve not to reply to it. A third was that she would be out, returning at the end of the afternoon, resulting in the same possibilities as above. A fourth possibility was that she and Viktor would devote a day or more to deciding whether to acknowledge the letter. He resolved, accordingly, that he would wait in his room against the first contingency; that he could safely leave his room if she did not telephone before two, until, say, six; stay on until eight, and then go out for the evening, and come back in the hope that there would be a message for him.

There was no call, so at two he went to the lobby and got a map of the city from the concierge. The hotel was a dozen blocks from the waterfront. He opened the main door and went out into the bright sun and air which, he could feel, was not many weeks away from achieving arctic temperature. He walked with pleasure, observing the sanitized, blond, husky, healthy, solid people who inhabit Sweden. The colors, with the uniform stress on the dark yellow, were brilliantly lit by the afternoon sun, and when he arrived on Slottsbacken he could see the water, a Prussian blue; the background to what seemed like a traveling boat show, huge luxury cruise boats, tankers, freighters, sailing yachts, dinghies.

He quickened his step and reached the long quay, which rounded gently on the two-mile-long waterfront, ending in the protective mole on the northeast side. Every kind of boat was there, stern-to at the quay, European fashion; and he walked by, examining them as he went, large schooners, medium and small sloops, yawls, ketches, motor launches of every size. On most boats there was activity. A blond boy, fourteen or fifteen, oblivious to the wind, in shorts and T-shirt, sanding down the guardrails; an old man, stitching a torn sail; a young woman sorting out groceries. There were boats from a hundred foreign ports, flying a dozen foreign flags. He saw a trim American racing yawl. A boy of college age lay on the deck, his head bent over the stern light, with pliers and a screwdriver in one hand. His head was only inches away from the quay. Blackford paused:

"Are you American?"

"Yep." The boy didn't look up, concentrating on the elusive wire he was patching.

"Is your boat"—Blackford saw that it was called *Esmeralda*—"wintering here?"

"Nope."

"How long have you been here?"

At this point the young man looked up, with that distinctive wariness of youth. He would, or he would not, was the clear expression on his face, encourage a continuation of the dialogue. His beardless, even-featured, light-skinned, golden, tanned face was distorted by the presence between his teeth of a screw; hair tumbled over one of his eyes. Having decided, apparently, that Blackford was at least inoffensive, he removed the screw from his mouth and said, "I've been crewing for my dad. Sailed across in June, after the Bermuda race. Took in the Fastnet, and he decided to do some cruising in the Baltic. We're headed back to the Antilles but don't want to push off from England until after the hurricane season. We'll be leaving here tomorrow, should make it to Southampton in six, seven days. I'm taking the semester off. Want to come aboard?"

"Yes, sure." Blackford bounced over the after pulpit and sat down in the cockpit. "Thanks. Go ahead with the stern light. Do you need any help?"

"Tell you the truth, I've forgotten how this damned voltmeter works. Usually Dad handles it, or Danny, and they're out shopping. Have you ever used one?"

"Sure. What's your power supply?"

"Twelve volts."

Blackford got up, adjusted the knobs, pointed out the relevant dial, and extended the crocodile clips to the young man. "What's your name?"

"Peter. Peter Briscoe. My father is Stephen Briscoe." There was just the slightest suggestion that Stephen Briscoe was a name one might be expected to recognize. Blackford didn't.

"My name is Blackford Oakes."

"Hi." Blackford, at thirty-one, was just old enough to cause hesitation in an eighteen-year-old's feel for whether he should be addressed by his first name, or mistered. Safer the unadorned salutation.

Peter tested the electrical connection, found it active, and pulled a knife from the battered leather sheath on his belt, the marlinespike jutting out, and, still lying on his stomach, cut off a few inches of electric tape and wound it around the wire splice.

"There," he said, sitting up and smiling with some satisfaction. The wind ran through his lanky brown hair. His skin was evenly bronzed by a long summer of sun.

"Want a beer or anything? Coke?"

"No thanks," said Blackford. "Tell you what I'm looking for. I just got here, I have a couple of weeks of unexpected vacation. I'd like to charter a boat."

"Sailboat?"

"Yeah."

"Bareboat?"

"No. I'd like a hand."

"Why?" Peter smiled. "You can work a voltmeter."

Blackford returned the smile. "Somebody who knows some of the good cruising spots, who speaks a little English or German, and can wash the dishes."

"You won't have any trouble. Not now, not mid-September. You need to speak to the harbormaster, name's Olaf, as in King Olaf. He knows every boat, the works."

"Do most of the hands speak English?"

"Yah, vee speek da English some bit." The boy did the imitation with natural enthusiasm. "Tell you what, I'll come with you. I can spot Olaf. We've been dealing with him all summer. Dad took him out one evening, and we carried him ashore three hours and two bottles of aquavit later, nice guy, even when he's zonked."

"That would be great." Within the hour it was arranged: The *Hjordis*, a forty-four-foot chalk-white cutter, with roller reefing, a full set of sails; a Dutch steel boat, snugly fitted out, with two berths in the forecastle, two in the main saloon, and a pipe berth aft of the icebox. Peter spent an hour on the local charts, indicating anchorages, inlets, stretches of water he and his father had especially taken to during their month's exploration. Sam, the mate, was uneasy in English but fluent in German. He was a widower at sixty, a retired fisherman. The simple papers were executed, and Blackford put down a fifty-dollar deposit, against the daily rate of fifty dollars. He could have the boat, Sam said, as long as he liked. Blackford told him he would come around in the morning and, followed by Peter, sprang onto the wharf, and headed back toward the *Esmeralda*. Impulsively Blackford said, "I'll have that beer now, if it's still available."

"Sure." With one leap, Peter traveled from the quay into the cockpit well, his hand breaking the fall by clutching adroitly the overhanging boom. The next step brought him down the companionway, and ten seconds later he arrived with a beer and a Coca-Cola. As they drank, Peter became voluble. They had had a very frightening dismasting during the Fastnet race. "Son of a gun damn near fell on Dad's head. We had to use the wire cutters to keep it from bashing in the hull. Real mess. Three competitors went right by us, just waved, that's all. Took four hours for the British coast guard to reach us. Real cool. They even insisted on towing the mast to Lands End—'menace to navigation,' they said. The new one is aluminum, did you notice? They call it an 'extrusion,' how do you like that? There were eight of us racing, now we're going back just the three of us. Here to Southampton, then the Azores, then the long one, to Grenada."

"How far is that?"

"2190 miles, from Ponta Delgada."

"How much water do you have?"

"Hundred and twenty gallons."

"Fuel."

"Same. Enough for about 150 hours of power. We won't use that much, we figure to hit the trades beginning a few hundred miles south of the Azores."

Without knowing what made him ask the question, Blackford suddenly said, "Peter, what would you say if the Russians fired off a satellite before we did?"

"A satellite what?"

"A satellite—something they succeeded in launching high enough and fast enough to escape gravity, and—you know—achieve perpetual motion around the earth."

"Hm. I'd say somebody's ass in Washington would be in a sling."

"Why?"

"I'm not a science major. I even have trouble with voltmeters." He grinned and tilted his head back to empty the Coca-Cola bottle. "But I mean, isn't science sort of *our* thing? I always think of the Russians in terms of lots of heavy tanks and artillery and millions of them dying chasing Napoleon and Hitler out, and freezing to death because Stalin says so. Maybe if they fire off a satellite it's because they stole the secrets from us? That's how they got the atom bomb, isn't it?"

"Well, sort of. But the Russians are pretty bright people."

"I hope so. Next term, ugh, I've got to read Dostoevski, Tolstoi, and the other guy, what's his name."

"Gogol? Turgenev?"

"I forget, but my roommate took the course last spring, freshman year, and he practically had to give up everything else, including sex. Everywhere he went you'd see him with a *huge* paperback"—Peter stretched out his arms—"and one day he looked at me, and said, 'Go ahead and laugh, but it'll be *you* next year.' Maybe I can find a sort of *Reader's Digest* version."

"That's one possibility."

"What's the other?"

"That you'll enjoy them."

And that, Blackford knew instantly, had been a disastrous breach of protocol. He had sounded patronizing. Things could never again be quite the same between him and Peter. In any event it was time to go. He got up.

"Peter, thanks. You were good help and good company. I'll look in on you tomorrow on the way to the *Hjordis*."

"Good night, Mr. Oakes." Peter rose, and extended his hand to help Blackford over to the quay, as if Blackford was an old man, like the Russian literature professor at college.

Chapter 32

HE WAS BACK in his hotel room at six, and the telephone rang a half hour later. He'd make the preliminaries easier for her:

"This is Julian. Tamara?"

"Yes."

"I am very glad you called."

"I have been at the hospital, with Viktor."

Blackford tensed. "Something . . . some fresh problem?"

"Surgery. Cosmetic surgery. The right eye."

"Is he . . . otherwise all right? I mean . . . heart, blood, that sort of thing?"

"He will be all right."

"How long will he be in the hospital?"

"Two weeks."

"Two weeks." Blackford's voice betrayed his disappointment. "Can I see you both then?"

"What about?"

"I need to see you and Viktor. It's . . . personal."

"We have an agreement with the Swedish Government. We are to report to the Foreign Ministry any attempts by Soviet *or* American agents to communicate with us."

"I am not here as an agent of any government."

"I don't believe our hosts would allow us to take your word"—the unintended harshness was quickly mitigated—"or anybody else's on the question."

"Tamara, what I am telling you is true. I am on leave of absence without pay. I have tentatively tendered my resignation. Nobody knows I am here. I think you can in good conscience consider this a purely personal contact."

"I shall have to think about that. Anyway, you could not under any circumstances see Viktor before two weeks."

"I'll return in two weeks."

"That means you are *required* to see him."

"No, Tamara. It means that I will adjust my plans so as to make a meeting possible. During the two weeks I intend to cruise."

"Where?"

"In a sailboat. In this area."

"I shall have to discuss the whole matter with Viktor, but I don't want to bring it up until after the operation."

"Let's leave it this way. In two weeks I'll send you another message. Will you call me then?"

Her voice softened a little, and she said, "All right. But you had better make that three weeks. Good-bye, Julian."

Blackford roamed the streets aimlessly, his attention infuriatingly fugitive. What *did* he want to speak to Viktor about? Why hadn't he succeeded in forcing himself to crystallize his thinking on this point? He tried the smorgasbord at the Opera Källaren, and managed three shots of aquavit, but he found it difficult to distract himself. He was asking himself such questions as: Is it a lie to decline to tell the truth? Or, more exactly: Is it a lie to decline to intervene with the truth? He supposed that the absolutists —he remembered Kant and St. Augustine in that context—would have said instantly, 'Yes.' But then they would simply not have approved of covert operations under any circumstances, so of what use were they? Against Lenin? Hitler? Stalin?

He returned to his hotel room and took comfort, as he so often did, from semiscientific absorptions. He had brought the Nautical Almanac for 1957, and set out to calculate exactly the times of sunrise and sunset the next day, the thirteenth, at his location. His eyes turned to the chart . . . Latitude 59° 20′ north, longitude 18° 5′ east. He refamiliarized himself with the almanac, entered the figures, and extracted the interpolations. The sun would rise at

5:17–6:17 daylight time, which was local time; and, for all the talk of the land of the perpetual light, the sun would set, according to the almanac, at 7:15 daylight time, notwithstanding that technically there was still a week of summer ahead. While he was at it, he computed the hour at which the sun would pass overhead at his meridian: 12:43 local time. Well, he would rise early, and put down anchor early. He showered, and took a book to bed, Ayn Rand's *Atlas Shrugged*. He had read, and enjoyed, *The Fountainhead*, and this sequel to it had been advertised as the revolt of the meritocracy against statism. He was attracted to experimental forms of nonorganized opposition to tyranny, and so he waded in, and was soon asleep.

Blackford had been sleeping several hours when, at 0300 GMT aboard the *Indianapolis,* Captain Y. Upsilon Jones, although he had begun drinking only at 0242, was rapidly approaching blotto. Lieutenant Plummer, at the wheel, had made the critical turn, and the collision was calculated for 0243, at which point Jenks received the frenzied signal from the radio operator. He yelled out *"Hard right rudder!"* to Plummer, then grabbed the intercom and in a hoarse whisper shouted to the perspiring captain, waiting in his cabin for the word to sound the general alarm:

"It's off! Abort! Came in uncoded!"

Jones gulped, relieved beyond measure—yet somehow wistful.

"What exactly was the message?"

"'URGENT INDIANAPOLIS ABORT ABORT ABORT WILL CONFIRM VIA IZN.' A few seconds later Stagg brings in the code. I'll bring it down."

By the time Jenks arrived, Captain Jones had opened the safe, bringing out simultaneously the code book and a fresh bottle of bourbon. He poured the bourbon first, then addressed himself to transcribing the terse code.

"CONFIRMING INSTRUCTIONS ABORT SCHEDULED MISSION. PROCEED PRESENT COURSE PENDING INSTRUCTIONS 1300 GMT. CINCLANT BURKE."

The two men were slouched in the two armchairs.

Captain Jones emptied his first glass. "Shee*yit!* What in *hell's* going on. We set ourselves up for a real cozy operation—"

Jenks interrupted him: "—and they're crazy enough to call it off?"

Captain Jones burped.

Jenks, twirling his glass, said: "I doubt poor Plummer will ever be the same again."

"One of these days he'll break security, you bet. He'll tell his cronies at the locker room about the night—"

Jenks interrupted him again. "Don't worry about it, Uppy. They won't believe him." He paused. ". . . Come to think of it, Uppy, might not be a bad idea if tomorrow you tell Stagg and Plummer the whole thing was an exercise, we knew about it ahead of time, but went through the"—he hated the word, but Uppy loved it, and it was a way of attracting him to any idea—"the simulations."

"Ah yes." Y. Upsilon Jones straightened up in his chair. "I already thought of that. Tomorrow, first thing."

Chapter 33

THREE WEEKS LATER BLACKFORD OAKES had excreted the lesser poisons of civilization: He went without liquor, fried foods, starchy desserts, late nights, sedentary days, hectic polemicizing. The weather, except for the two-day storm during which he and Sam took shelter in the tight harbor at Vispy, had been crisp, cloudless, bracing: twelve hours a day of salt air and bright colors and the sweet sounds of sea-plowing and wind-whistling, followed by stillness. Every morning Sam, having looked at the barometer and the telltale, would suggest the day's outing, and except for the long run to Gotland at the end of the first week, he kept the *Hjordis* in waters in which she could take quick protection. Everywhere, in that water warren streaked by hills and grassy slopes, and little white farms and summer cottages, there were bights into whose loose embrace you could ease up, drop anchor, and experience instantly the sedative relief of the lee shore. There were here and there tiny slips, into one of which every other day Blackford would ease the cutter in, tie up, and walk with Sam to the local supply and grocery store, and occasionally take on water. He doubted they had used ten gallons of fuel during the twenty days, so generous were the winds, and so adroit Sam's maneuvering. In the evening Sam lit the little coal stove, and cooked. Usually it was fish, and usually Blackford or Sam had caught it. Blackford knew nothing about ichthyology: He could distinguish between a whale and a sardine, but everything in between was a blur, and so he needed to feign enthusiasm when Sam would announce excitedly, after Blackford had landed a fish, that that was a whatever, splendid-to-eat. And indeed it inevitably was splendid to eat. Fish and lemon and hard rolls and cheese and oranges and apples and, at breakfast, the strongest coffee Blackford had ever tasted outside of Turkey, coffee Sam took proprietary pride in making, putting in Blackford's mug the exact amount of sugar Sam deemed appropriate.

Sam talked about his career in Norway, as a commercial fisherman, and about his conscription by the Nazis during the war. They had put a superannuated German sergeant on board Sam's fishing vessel, which now had two functions, to bring in fish, the whole catch to be turned over to the Germans, who then remitted to Sam a salary the equivalent of a German corporal's; and the supplementary duty—to report on any shipping activity. To expedite this, Sam said, they had equipped his small boat with a sturdy radar, which had served him well after the war until, finally, it decomposed, but at about the same time, his wife had insisted they move to Stockholm where she could look after her senescent mother, who adamantly refused to leave the land of her birth. Sam used the proceeds from the sale of his boat to buy a little house on the water a few miles from Stockholm. As it happened the mother-in-law outlived the wife, and it was Sam who was at the bedside when the old lady finally died. The house was lonely, so he took in a young couple, clerks in the state-owned liquor store, who kept him company. He looked after the *Hjordis* for its owner, a cosmopolitan and permissive businessman who spent much of the year outside Sweden, leaving the *Hjordis* to Sam to maintain and to charter out. The German sergeant who had spent the war on Sam's boat—transmitting, by radio, coded information on adventitious encounters at sea with foreign vessels, and checking to see that the full catch of fish was duly turned over to the German quartermaster—had been ambushed by the resistance during the last days of the occupation, and shot. Sam said he felt very sorry about this, because Hans was an old German, not at all like the Nazis. Blackford would sometimes tune out during Sam's soliloquies; but Sam, even when he noticed, didn't really mind. He was enjoying the opportunity to revisit his use of the German tongue;

and besides, had taken a strong liking to the fresh and fetching American, whose graceful movements about the cutter, and keen interest in the details of its operation, excited paternal instincts in Sam, who was childless. It was not long before Sam discerned that Blackford was engaged in something other than a mere outing.

Sam could hardly fail to notice the concentrated austerity of Blackford's regime. Blackford's naked plunge into the cold seawater in the morning, and again in the late afternoon after they had anchored, was never failing, not even during the storm. After the second day Sam no longer went through the motions of offering Blackford a drink from the store of aquavit and beer, and at nights, while Sam sat in the main saloon (Blackford elected to sleep forward, in the fo'c'sle), listening to the radio and smoking, he would focus on the light shining down from the kerosene lamp on the bulkhead from which Blackford read. The cabin door was always open, giving Sam a view of Blackford's head, and the book that rested on his sweater, with which he warded off the night's chill. Sam noticed that sometimes an hour or more would go by, and no page would turn, even though Blackford was wide awake as witness that occasionally he would even call out to Sam—a civil effort at conviviality?—a remark about the music being broadcast; a question about the content of a Norwegian news broadcast; whatever. But Sam doubted he could be helpful to Mr. Oakes in wrestling with whatever Mr. Oakes was wrestling with—a girl, most probably—but where was the girl who would spurn such a man? So Sam devoted himself to wresting from the *Hjordis* everything she had. He would wait until the last moment to reef the mainsail, or contract the headsail. He took pains to steer Blackford to Sam's most private reserves, the two or three hidden inlets to which he never escorted those of his charterers who were . . . unfeeling. The deepwater run to Gotland had been one of those magical passages, superb, spellbinding, with wind, speed, sound, color, waves, interacting in exuberant harmony, the landfall at Kappelshamm coinciding with the setting of the sun, a seventy-mile passage begun before daybreak, in a following sea, with the storm spinnaker set all the way. That night Mr. Oakes had shown great animation as he ate his fish, his cheese, his apple, and drank the cold pure water from the container in the icebox. Mr. Oakes had said that one day, maybe soon, he would like to come back to *Hjordis,* with a friend—he did not specify the sex— but would only do so on the condition that Sam was still with the *Hjordis,* and there and then he wrote down Sam's address and telephone number, and Sam was very pleased—proud, even.

Five days later they were back in Stockholm. They reached the quay at four and, thoroughly proficient by this time, Blackford backed the cutter under power expertly, after dropping the anchor two boat-lengths out into the bay. A little boy accepted the tossed docking lines and cleated them diagonally to the docking posts, as nonchalantly as though he were a professional seaman. Blackford's seabag was packed and, wearing his rugged sweater and topsiders, he extended his hand to the man for whom he had already written out the check, and said, "Thank you, Sam. I almost envy that German sergeant who spent so much time with you at sea." Sam smiled, and said, electing for the first time to speak in broken English, "You come soon again, Mr. Oakes."

Blackford jumped up to the quay, using the after pulpit as fulcrum, and Sam passed over the seabag and, pipe in mouth, waved a stoical good-bye.

Chapter 34

AFTER CHECKING in at Reception, Blackford went to the gift shop, bought a waterproof watch for Sam, scribbled out a note, and addressed the envelope. He took a second sheet of paper and wrote a simple note to Tamara. "Am back, and waiting for your call, Room 322. Julian." He gave the letter and the parcel to the concierge and went up to his room, to which his bags had been delivered, and placed a call to his mother in London. She received him, as always, affectionate and solicitous. He remembered to ask after his stepfather who, it transpired, was well, notwithstanding the episodic offensives of gout. Blackford then tensed to ask the question whether there were messages for him.

"Yes," said Lady Sharkey, a cable had arrived that very morning. "I opened it, of course, but it doesn't mean anything to me. It must be *very* secret, darling."

"Read it to me, Mother—whom is it signed by?"

"Well, that's mystifying, too, because the whole thing, including the signature, is in numbers. You know, like 1-2-3-4-5?"

"Well, Mother, does it say where it was sent from?"

"It was sent from Poughkeepsie, New York, at eight o'clock last night."

"How long is it?"

"Do you mean, dear, how many numbers?"
"Well, yes."
"I would say about fifty."
"Mother, would you mind terribly just dictating those numbers to me? Dictate in lots of three numbers, and I'll repeat them."
"Of course I don't mind, dear, but are you sure you wouldn't want me to take this down to the cable office and forward it?"
"No no no. I have a pad of paper. Go ahead."
It wasn't that much of an operation, actually; in five minutes it was done.

In reply to her inevitable question, Blackford said he would make every effort to stop by London on his way back to the States, but could not promise either that he would manage or even predict exactly when he might get to London, assuming he did. She sounded warm and well and, as always after talking with her, reaching back to the dawn of childhood memory, Blackford felt refreshed for having done so; better disposed.

The cable was clearly intended for Viktor.

Blackford, stretched out on the couch, was catching up on the newsmagazines at the moment the telephone rang. Her voice this time was effusively hospitable. "Viktor had a letter from Vadim. Ever since, we have been waiting for your message. To hell with the Swedish authorities. Can you come to dinner?"

"Of course. But shouldn't we meet at a restaurant? For privacy?"

"Viktor's family are out of town. The house is empty. Come to us at seven."

Blackford showered, dressed in his tweed suit, and resolved to walk toward the waterfront before hailing a taxi. Would he ever, he wondered, overcome the pedigreed suspiciousness? Here he was, in a neutral area of the world, after three weeks of desultory cruising in Swedish waters. The probability that he was being followed approached zero. Still, he was going to Viktor; and therefore he would be careful. Even at the risk of being objectively ridiculous. Who, after all, would know that he was being ridiculous? His evasive action was a matter between him and a psychiatrist to fret over, when the moment came to consult a psychiatrist, if that moment came.

And so, well down the avenue, he flagged a cab.

The house on Malmö Street was substantial. Blackford knew nothing of the business of Viktor's brother-in-law. But clearly he was well established. The house stood back from the street behind a grilled iron fence that seemed to surround the whole property and, though of moderate dimensions, was massively constructed, the Swedish ocher-colored stone rising up the three stories to the gabled roof. The gate was open and Blackford crossed the little lawn, went up the stone steps, and rang the doorbell. It was opened by Tamara. She was dressed in a silk shirt over which she wore a fine, light, cream-colored sweater, the mother-of-pearl buttons unfastened, and a midnight-blue pleated skirt. Her hair, streaked with white, was neatly braided in the Scandinavian fashion, twined around her head. Blackford extended his hand. She took it and then, with both hands, drew his head to her, and kissed him lightly on the forehead.

She took him then by the hand, and led him into the living room, where the fire was lit. Opposite sat Viktor. Blackford had dreaded the prospect of looking at Viktor's face. He was agreeably surprised, but Viktor noticed the hesitation.

"Come, Julian." He bent over so that the light from the table lamp starkly illuminated his features. "You may examine my face. Everyone else has done so in the past few weeks. You will find it is not all that easy to mutilate a graduate of Vorkuta."

Plainly Viktor was pleased with the work done in Stockholm by the facial surgeon, and Blackford found it necessary to deduce which of the two eyes was glass—from the evanescing little scar-grid that surrounded the eye area that had been operated on (the two eyes turned in unison). Viktor had let his hair grow out, and though it was very nearly white, it was there, thick and raffish in contrast to the close-cropped Viktor Kapitsa of Chantilly. Viktor had grown a beard, whether for cosmetic or other reasons Blackford did not know. Viktor stood up without suggestion of effort. But when he walked over toward the bureau to fetch a drink, there was a limp.

Tamara addressed her husband in Russian. After a moment's hesitation he stopped, and turned; and went back to the sofa, sitting down. "Tamara insists on serving us. What will you have?"

"What are you having?"

"We are both so happy to see you, we have brought up my sister's French champagne. Do you like champagne?"

"I will drink champagne with you and Tamara anytime."

Viktor smiled and nodded toward Tamara. To Blackford he said:

"Let me say it once, and then not repeat it. I know that Vadim, my beloved Vadim, put you in a most difficult position. I am sure you do not want to talk about it, and I am in no position to make professional judgments. As a human being, I thank you for saving me and Tamara."

Blackford's eyes swelled, and he managed with difficulty to acknowledge the toast and, after Viktor and Tamara had drunk, raised his own glass, deferentially. On the last days of his solitary cruise he had come to realize that in fact he needed no help from Viktor in analyzing his own problem. *That* deck, that terrible mix of duties, compulsions, affections, only he could shuffle into coherence. He had come to Stockholm, he realized as he held the course to Gotland, laboring to keep the spinnaker filled, to feast his eyes on one concrete accomplishment—Viktor alive: an accomplishment for which he had paid a professional price of incalculable scale. He wanted to convince himself that he had done—not the *right* thing (such terminology was extrinsic, he increasingly realized, to the trade he practiced) but to convince himself that he had done something he was not *ashamed* to have done. All that this required, he finally apprehended aboard the *Hjordis,* was to see him, Viktor—them, Viktor and Tamara—together; alive; mending—free. The fireplace crackled, and the champagne was poured yet again. Suddenly Blackford remembered the cable. He reached into his pocket.

"Viktor. There was a cable waiting for me at my mother's house in London—the only address I left in Washington. It's got to be from Vadim to you. Vadim obviously didn't want to send any cryptography directly to this address. But no one in his right mind would attempt to harass my mother," Blackford smiled as he extended the note pad, "though no doubt M1-5's cryptanalysts are out in force."

Viktor put on his eyeglasses and studied the numbers. He smiled, as he drew on his fabled memory, and pulled out a pencil. He read out the message in Russian. And then translated it: "VIKTOR: FOTO REVEALS ROCKET MOVED TO LAUNCHING PAD OCTOBER 3 VADIM."

"That means," Viktor said with a sigh, laying down his cigar, "they are ready to fire at any moment. It would appear to mean that the purchased American machine has succeeded in activating the transistors." He looked up, with a twinkle in his eye, and raised his forefinger mischievously to his lips:

"I've got a secret!" he smiled.

Blackford laughed. "Oh no! Here we go again."

"When they fire the PS—that is how they designate it at Tyura Tam—they plan to let it circle the globe a full twenty-four hours before making an announcement. This is to make certain it is in stable condition before giving it publicity. And *I*"—he spoke now in little-boy whispers—"know the frequencies PS will transmit on—20.005 and 40.002 megacycles—wavelength 1.5 and 7.5."

Viktor rose and went to a large shortwave radio perched near the window. "When I am through listening to the broadcasts on this radio, I have customarily left the dial at 20.005. From now on I will do that—but *also* leave on the power." He flicked on the switch, and there was crackling of static until he squelched down the noise.

Viktor returned to his chair. Thereafter the evening flowed like the champagne: It was as if the three had grown up together. No subject was too personal to touch on. Viktor spoke of one of his scientific companions, Mirtov, who had gone a month ago to the hospital at Tyura Tam—*demanding* to see Viktor, walking right by administrators, doctors, nurses, sitting down finally by Viktor's bedside with a box of sweets and a book he had purchased in Paris. Viktor laughed: "If they had done anything to Mirtov, Korolev himself would quit! And that would be the end of the project!"

Blackford asked, over coffee and brandy, why the same reasoning did not apply to Viktor.

"My offenses were too egregious. And my theoretical contributions to the PS were done, although they could have kept me very busy indeed, because I feel great energy now, and my scientific resources are not exhausted, no, not by any means. When you return to America, Julian, you may tell that to your friends. I am happy when I am working. I am happy when I am in Russia. But now that I will not be in Russia again, I will be happy working elsewhere, and now there will be extra-scientific satisfactions we will take from our work—am I correct, Tamara?" She nodded. They were holding hands on the sofa, and were holding hands still when, two hours later, they bade Blackford good night, and a bon voyage, having told him Viktor would, in the next month or two, be in touch with Vadim to make arrangements for emigrating to the United States. Blackford left the house but did not ask for a taxi. He wanted to walk home, to float home in the cold air, warmed aloft by high spirits. He could not remember when last he felt better. It was after midnight before he reached the hotel. In bed, he fell quickly asleep.

At 4:32 in the morning the telephone rang. It was Tamara. "Julian, come quickly!"

Blackford's voice was panicked. "Is Viktor all right?"

"Yes, yes, but come!"

"All right. I'll be right there."

He jiggled the receiver, and got finally the sleepy voice at Reception. He demanded a taxi. "*Immediately*. This is an emergency."

In less than five minutes, wearing sailing sweater and corduroy pants, Blackford was at the hotel entrance. He gave the address to the waiting taxi, and fifteen minutes later bounded out through the gate up to the big oaken door, and rang.

"Come in, come in!" Tamara whispered. She led him into the dark living room, lit by a single lamp. There at the far end of the room, sitting in silence, was Viktor. But there were sounds. Sibilant, clear, self-confident staccato sounds in three very rapid bursts, split-second pause, and repeat, pause, repeat. *Beep-beep-beep. Beep-beep-beep. Beep-beep-beep.*

They all listened for minutes in silence before Viktor spoke.

"I had the radio at my bedside. It woke us at 4:15. It is one hour later at Tyura Tam. The launch must have been at approximately 4:05 local time." Viktor looked at his watch. "In a few minutes we will not hear it. In a half hour we will hear it again. The planetary revolution will take one hour and thirty-five minutes. This, Julian, is the most important moment in scientific history since the discovery of flight." He uttered those words without entirely concealing a certain progenitive pride.

Blackford paused, instinctively and genuinely deferential to the epochal deed. But then he said: "Viktor. I must go quickly to the hotel. The least I can do under the circumstances is alert Washington."

"Use my telephone."

"No. I'd be acting officially, the call might be monitored, and you might get into trouble with the Swedes. I told the taxi to wait. Thank you for calling me." He found himself embracing Viktor and kissing Tamara. "I'll see you again" were his last words.

* * *

At his hotel room he roused the operator and gave her the home telephone number of Anthony Trust in New York. The call went through without interruption. At a few minutes after midnight Trust was still awake.

"It's Black."

"Well, and what pleasure dome are you calling in from, my friend?"

Anthony had obviously been drinking.

"Listen, and listen hard, okay?"

Anthony's reply came as after an ice-cold shower. "I'm listening."

"Who is on first," Blackford spoke slowly, emphatically.

Trust's guttural reaction revealed he hadn't forgotten the code. But Blackford, in his excitement, elaborated. "It's up and functioning." And then to business. "Got a pencil? Two zero point zero zero five and four zero point zero zero two megs. This is a twenty-four-hour . . . twenty-three-hour . . . beat, for whatever it's worth."

A husky voice replied: "Well, it's worth whatever a doctor is worth who alerts you you have twenty-three hours to live. Where are you calling from?"

"Never mind. Over and out. Good night."

* * *

Twelve hours later aboard the overnight flight (Stockholm–Gander–New York–Washington) Blackford looked out over the darkening North Sea. He wondered idly whether, at that moment, the *Sputnik* was at its apogee of 947 kilometers (Viktor's fine-tuned declaration), or at its perigee of 228 kilometers. Either way, he comforted himself, it would not be bumping into SAS's four-propped Constellation. It would, he shut his eyes to perform the arithmetic, take the Swedish airliner eleven hours to travel a distance the *Sputnik* would travel in—twelve minutes.

I'll be damned.

Tomorrow in Washington would be chaotic. Tomorrow, *everywhere* would be chaotic. Just think, Oakes, you might have been born Japanese, in which case you'd have had an easy out: You'd commit hara-kiri!

Another thing, Oakes—you might have been Russian. In which case *they'd* have performed the hara-kiri on *you!*

Or is hara-kiri a transitive verb? He beckoned the stewardess for another drink.

Can someone *perform* hara-kiri on someone else? Surely not; it must be a . . . reflexive verb? Or is it a verb at all? A simple noun, surely? He might, when taken to the office of the Director, interrupt him to ask whether he happened to know the answer to that question.

Blacky wondered what it would be like when he stepped forward to confess: "It wasn't only Vadim who knew. I also knew."

Beep-beep-beep. Beep-beep-beep. Beep-beep-beep.

What does it say? Is there a symbolic meaning in that defiant cluster of sounds which, beginning tomorrow, will electrify, serenade, importune, threaten—the whole world? Is there a cryptographic key?

Blackford tilted his seat back, and slowly closed his eyes. His mind wandered.

His lips gradually parted: and soon there was a silent triumphant smile.

His fantasy enthralled him. He pinched it in all its erogenous zones. It *sang* out with pleasure! (He beckoned the stewardess for another drink.) Yes. The next day, after his auto-da-fé in the Director's office, he would say: "But sir, you may not have heard! CIA-Stockholm *has broken the Russian code!* That *Sputnik,* gamboling about the universe like a young gazelle, *is out of control!*!** Russian scientists are *working* f-e-v-e-r-i-s-h-l-y to force it to change its signal before its meaning is DISCOVERED!!

"But the CIA—through one of its young, resourceful (to-be-sure not *altogether* predictable) agents—HAS ALREADY BROKEN THE CODE!"

"What! What! What!" the Director would surely say.

To which Blackford Oakes would most solemnly reply: "That *Sputnik,* careening loose-footedly about the planet, paddycakin' 'round and 'round and 'round the spheres, is singing out to all the people of the world a fugitive cry of joy, *decoded by the CIA!* It is saying, over and over again,

"'I CHOSE FREEDOM!'

"Isn't that great . . . sir?"

Epilogue

THE ASTRONAUT had been assiduously briefed as to his conduct upon becoming the first human being to set foot on the moon. The President had insisted that his own speechwriters should compose the message which—he predicted, leaning back in his chair in the Oval Office—would "resonate through the echo chambers of time"; from which the head of the National Aeronautics and Space Administration deduced that the President wanted something at once awed and awesome, exuberant and spiritual, heroic and lyrical.

The President had so instructed his chief speechwriter. Moreover, all other communications from the astronaut were to be of a purely functional nature, to heighten the melodrama.

"We don't want the guy who first steps on the moon, 22 billion U.S. bucks having been spent on him, to say, with everybody in the world listening, that he owes it all to Aunt Tillie." President Nixon had been intimately involved in the selection of the first moon-landing astronaut, reviewing personal history, studying his physical features; and indeed—the world seemed to agree on that tense morning at Cape Kennedy when at 9:32 the huge missile discharged what seemed a century's pent-up energy, trembling its way up to the unknown—the first man on the moon might have been sculpted by Walt Disney himself, to play opposite Snow White.

But although a highly disciplined scientist, engineer, athlete, and —if need be—martyr, the astronaut, setting down his nearly weightless boot on the sands of the moon, having given out the wrought-iron message crafted by a dozen hands—something to do about a large step forward for mankind—was overcome by a flush of gratitude, and he blustered chattily to his two companions, one of them standing by in the space module, a few feet away. But the radioed words would travel to him via Houston, Texas, a half-million-mile round trip; then greetings to the other astronaut, guiding the capsule in orbit about the moon, on whose orderly reflexes hung the chances of returning safely to earth. Then—in defiance of explicit instructions—he spoke a word of affection for his wife and son.

But on doing so, violating explicit instructions, he experienced a flash of remorse, and so he resolved to try to salvage the situation, by professionalizing his breach of discipline: so he went on to congratulate "everyone" at Houston Control.

But having done that, once again the personal fit was on him, and so he blurted out: "Especially Punky and Viktor." Walter Cronkite, to be sure only after a few seconds' research, supplied the background of the two men to the avid audience.

Ninety percent of the world's population (it had been officially estimated six years earlier) knew of the death of John F. Kennedy two hours after the event. About the landing of a human being on the moon the figures were comparable; but the 10 percent of the world's population who did not learn quickly about the moon landing came to about 60 million people, and one of those was Blackford Oakes: who, in Borneo, was engaged in a preliminary survey of a long-distance radar-detection site deep in the interior.

It had been a grisly trip, in jungle heat on the first leg out to the highland, and back through jungle heat on the leg back to the settlement at Balikpapan, where, descending from the jeep at the hotel, Blackford Oakes gave instructions to the driver and walked wearily up the dilapidated steps, parting the screen to enter the hotel lobby, with the ceiling fan that brought grudging movement to the fetid air.

The concierge greeted him in German, handing him the contents of his room key locker, accumulated during the week of his absence.

There was a telegram. As the concierge shuffled through assorted packages to see if there was anything more, Blackford ripped open the envelope: "M. BLACKFORD OAKES C/O HOTEL SUHARNO, BALIKPAPAN, BORNEO, HOLD FOR ARRIVAL. BLACKFORD: RE YOUR COMMUNICATION OF OCTOBER 4, 1957, DON'T GIVE IT ANOTHER THOUGHT. WHAT'S ON SECOND. LOVE ANTHONY."

Acknowledgments

I am as ever indebted to more people than I can manageably name. But I must once again especially thank Sophie Wilkins for her perceptive reading. Samuel S. Vaughan and Betty Prashker, though they are ever so high and mighty with Doubleday (and with me), were never too busy to advise and encourage. My brother F. Reid Buckley gave me invaluable help, and my son Christopher administered corrections in that authoritative style to which he became accustomed as a child. Again, Joseph Isola is responsible for the fine copyreading. Dorothy McCartney's research was indispensable, as also Frances Bronson's editorial coordination. And, once again, I am inexpressibly grateful to Mr. Alfred Aya, Jr., of San Francisco for the technical aid. When he was a little boy, forty years ago, Alfred used to amuse himself by tiptoeing out of his room to the hotel elevators and rewiring them, so that when you pushed UP, you went DOWN. Thus, if you wanted to go up to the tenth floor, you found yourself on . . . first. He has not entirely grown up. For which, I repeat, my gratitude.

W.F.B.

Stamford, Connecticut
July 1979